Geometrical psychology, or, The science of representation : an abstract of the theories and diagrams of B. W. Betts – Primary Source Edition

Cook, Louisa S

GEOMETRICAL PSYCHOLOGY

OR

THE SCIENCE OF REPRESENTATION

AN ABSTRACT OF THE

THEORIES AND DIAGRAMS

OF

B W BETTS

BY

LOUISA S COOK

LONDON

GEORGE REDWAY

YORK STREET COVENT GARDEN

1887

19. A. 131.

CONTENTS.

DIAGRAMS.

Part I.

Part II.

PREFACE.

———◆◇◆———

BENJAMIN BETTS was born in the year 1832. He
was educated in England as an architect, and showed
considerable promise of success; but no system of
architecture not fully based on mathematics could
satisfy him, and he felt that decorative art should not
be altogether arbitrary and conventional, nor yet a
slavish reproduction of natural forms, but should be
executed with understanding according to sound principles of scientific conventionalisation. His mind
turned towards the study of internal truth, and he
resolved to quit his intended career in order to think
out his philosophy of life. He went abroad to secure
the quiet and freedom from distraction which the
abstruse nature of his studies required, but the
solitude in which he has lived, while aiding his spiritual
conceptions, has proved a hindrance when he wished
to give out the result of his thought to the world, for
having lived so much apart from men it has become
very difficult for him to make his ideas intelligible to
others

After spending some time in India and the East, he
obtained a post in the Government Civil Service, at
Auckland, New Zealand, as Trigonometrical Computor

of the Survey Department. From this* he draws a modest income which enables him to devote all his leisure time to the metaphysical studies he delights in. The study of internal truth by degrees connected itself in his mind with ideas of form, which combination was probably the result of his early training in Decorative and Architectural Art. An analogy used by Fichte in "The Science of Knowledge," of the correspondence of the line and the circle with modes of consciousness, led to his conception of the idea of developing a Science of Representation. He perceived with Leo Grindon that "all forms are representative, and their significance is the science of sciences." When he had succeeded in developing the plane forms which are his symbols of sense-consciousness, he sent them with a letter to Mr Ruskin, but Mr. Ruskin failed to perceive the intention of the diagrams, and replied that Art must be spontaneous, and could not be made mechanical, supposing that Mr. Betts was attempting some new departure in Art, not in metaphysical science. Later, when Mr. Betts had also developed the corolla forms, he sent the series of diagrams to his sister, with a manuscript in which he attempted to explain them to her. For, practically as well as theoretically, Mr. Betts holds the opinion that for all true work a union of the male and female mind is required. Miss Betts, though sincerely anxious to help and sympathise with her brother in his studies, had not the mathematical and metaphysical training which might have enabled her to be of service to

* Since the above was written Mr. Betts has relinquished his Government Post.

him, besides which Mr. Betts imagined that the significance of his representative forms was self-evident, so his manuscript was devoted rather to the outpouring of the emotion which the contemplation of the spiritual evolution of Man inspired in him than an accurate explanation of his system of symbology.

After the lapse of some time Mr. Betts's diagrams were sent to Mrs. George Boole, the widow of the mathematician. Mrs. Boole was much fascinated by the diagrams, rather from the mathematical than the metaphysical point of view. She carried on a long correspondence with Mr. Betts, and made some allusions to his work in a little book entitled " Symbolic Methods of Study," which she published in 1884. Also she showed the diagrams to many mathematical and scientific friends; among others to the late James Hinton and the late Mr Spottiswoode, President of the Royal Society, as well as to many artists. All allowed that Mr. Betts appeared to have got hold of some idea, but to discover exactly what it was required more labour and time than men immersed in important work of their own could give to it. Mr. Julian Hawthorne also was interested in Mr. Betts's work. He was on the point of starting for America when it was shown to him, so that he was not able to study it to any considerable extent, but he felt that even if it was not all that Mr. Betts claimed it to be, at least the work had a human interest, and ought to be preserved as being the life-work of an individual thinker.

Ultimately the present writer, seeing that no one more capable seemed likely to assist Mr. Betts in

preparing his work for publication, undertook to
make an abstract of it, having the necessary leisure,
though no special qualification for the work beyond
some natural bent of mind towards the study of
spiritual philosophy. Mr. Mohini M. Chatterji, a
grandson of the learned Rajah Rammohun Roy,
through his extensive acquaintance with Eastern philosophy, has been of the greatest help in clearing up
the obscurities of Mr. Betts's symbology So curiously
enough the leading idea of Mr. Betts's Science of
Life, that of polarity, finds a double illustration, for
not only has his male thought been taken up and completed by a woman, but his Western thought has also
found its complement and explanation in that of the
East Mr. Finch, Q C, late Fellow of Queen's and
Senior Wrangler, has also aided in the elucidation
of Mr. Betts's thought

THE SCIENCE OF REPRESENTATION.

PART I.

SECTION I.

SUBJECT PROPOSED.

THE diagrams which are considered in the following pages are the work of Mr. Benjamin Betts, of Auckland, New Zealand.

Mr. Betts has spent more than twenty years in studying the evolution of Man. He contemplates Man, not from the physical, but from the metaphysical point of view; thus the evolution of Man is for him the evolution of human consciousness. He attempts to represent the successive stages of this evolution by means of symbolical mathematical forms. These forms represent the course of development of human consciousness from the animal basis, the pure sense-consciousness, to the spiritual or divine consciousness; both which extremes are *not man*—the one underlying, the other transcending the limits of human evolution.

Mr. Betts felt that consciousness is the only fact that we can study directly, since all other objects of knowledge must be perceived through consciousness.

Mathematical form, he considers, is the first reflection and most pure image of our subjective activity. Then follows number, having a close relation to linear conception. Hence mathematical form with number supplies the fittest symbols for what Mr. Betts calls "The Science of Representation," the orderly representation by a system of symbolisation of the spiritual evolution of life, plane after plane. "Number," Philo said, "is the mediator between the corporeal and the incorporeal."

It may be objected that we have already a system of word-symbols for the purpose of Representation, and that therefore a system of linear mathematical symbols is superfluous. But words are inexact, arbitrary, uncertain, and especially so for the expression of metaphysical ideas. Such words as *substance*, *essence*, *passion*, are used in quite contrary senses by different people, or by the same person at different times. Mathematics is *par excellence* the exact science, and mathematical symbols cannot be loosely applied; they must be in strict correspondence with the thing signified, since otherwise the mind rejects them. But a true symbol when once the inner meaning is perceived is felt to be necessary, exact, satisfying. It can stand for that and nothing else— or rather only that and whatever else is merely the repetition of it on a different plane. Naturally mathematical diagrams are not capable of such wide and general application as words, but within their narrower limits they have greater depth, and they may be made of the greatest use in defining the meaning of scientific and metaphysical terms At least it must be granted that thought is stimulated and enriched by the development of an additional mode of expression

The symbolic forms which Mr. Betts has evolved

through his system of Representation resemble, when developed in two dimensions, conventionalised but very scientifically and beautifully conventionalised leaf-outlines. When in more than two dimensions they approximate to the forms of flowers and crystals.

These mathematical curves might serve as a truer and more scientific basis of classification for Botany than de Candolle's system or any other yet employed, many so-called amorphous developments of the Flora being readily reducible to law according to this method. For instance, the simple corollas, the horn-shaped corollas, and the bi-axial corollas would supply three main classes of flower forms, each of which might be divided into various distinct sub-classes.

The fact that he has accidentally portrayed plant-forms when he was studying human evolution is an assurance to Mr Betts of the fitness of the symbols he has developed, as it affords presumptive evidence that the laws he is studying intuitively admit of universal application.

SECTION II.

SCHEME OF EVOLUTION.

MR. BETTS's Representative diagrams trace the path of the monad through five planes or standing-grounds of human evolution. He commences from the animal basis, which he takes as the zero or starting-point of the human scale of progression, and proceeding onwards and upwards ends with that culmination of human possibilities when man becomes more than man, and his further evolution must be as a being on such a transcendent plane of existence that it might be called divine.

All attempts to trace the course of the evolution of life must begin at some point of the eternal circle. Mr. Betts has begun with the evolution of man, but the principles of evolution which he discovers through his studies apply equally to the evolutions of higher or lower forms of consciousness, and even to those planes of existence which we usually term inanimate Only by studying ourselves, he believes, can we ever arrive at a true knowledge of the external.

The starting-point of the human evolution is the animal sense-consciousness, which, though a positive plane of life for the lower animals, affords but a negative basis of consciousness for man. The symbolic representation of animal sense-consciousness is in two dimensions, and in form resembles a leaf whose apex is about equal to a right angle.

The first human standing-ground is that of rational sense-consciousness. Self-gratification is the predominant motive on this ground It is represented by a series of diagrams in two dimensions resembling leaf-forms. They are in pairs, of which those which he calls positive or male forms usually have an apex less than a right angle, and those which he calls female or negative an apex greater than a right angle

The second standing-ground is negative, the reaction from the first, which is positive. It is the ground of the lower morality. Will is developed as distinguished from the mere impulsive volition of the first ground. Self-control is the predominant motive. The dimensions of the form are contracted to a point which is now not a mere point of possibility as at first, but a focus of realised sensuous activity, repressed. Commonly, however, this ground consists rather in the circumscription than suppression of sensuous activity (the total suppression of sensuous activity would be death), which is now no longer allowed exercise for its own sake, but as a means to an end. Thus the representation of forms actually possible in life, instead of being a point will be a circle, or rather a circumference, for it is not necessarily a true circle.

The third standing-ground Mr. Betts calls the ground of spiritual activity, but it is rather psychical than truly spiritual, the spiritual evolution being that of the fifth ground Work is the motive of this ground. The sensuous activities are now allowed free exercise again, but as servants not as masters. The representative diagrams are in three dimensions, for the consciousness now has depth as well as surface extension In form they resemble the corollas of flowers, the male series trumpet-shaped, and the female series bell-shaped.

The fourth is again a negative standing-ground of life, the reaction from the third ground, as the second from the first It is the sacrifice of the personal Will, from which sacrifice it is re-born as a spiritual Will, in union with the divine or universal Will. Mr Betts professes himself unable to give any representation of life on this ground, since even the most advanced of ordinary humanity have scarcely entered upon it; also being a negative and reactionary ground it would be almost unrepresentable by diagram. The motive of this ground is a yearning for union with the infinite.

The fifth standing-ground is spiritual, the ground of intuitive knowledge. As the spiritual now becomes a positive plane of life it would be capable of representation if we were able to draw diagrams in four dimensions, but our present consciousness is limited to only three. Normal human beings have not yet attained to this plane of life, though the aspirations of a few tend thitherward; consequently no definite conception can be formed of such a condition, except by inference from the analogies and correspondences of lower planes of life, or through the revelation of higher beings who have already developed this grade of consciousness in themselves. It is the plane of the occult—what we with our limited ideas of nature call the Supernatural.

SECTION III.

THE GREAT DUALITY. EVOLUTION THROUGH POLARITY, ETC.

THE only attribute of a point is that it marks position. Take away this attribute and in the unposited point we have a symbol of pure Being, the abstract noumenon, that which underlies every mode of phenomenal manifestation, every form of existence. It is at once All and Nothing, at once Absolute Consciousness and Unconsciousness. All—since it contains the potentiality of everything, past, present, and to come. Nothing—since having no form, no limit, it is non-existent, *quoad nos*. It is Consciousness itself, and yet it is unconscious according to our conception of consciousness, for there is nothing beside itself for it to be conscious of—no differentiation of subject and object. That " Being must exist " Mr. Betts is obliged to postulate as the first law of evolution Manifestation is to arise. That Being may be manifest as existence the unposited point divides into two, the great Alpha and Omega, the first polarisation of Being. He represents this duality as a circuit of activity proceeding from a point and a circumferential

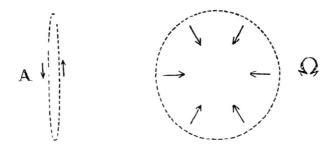

activity tending towards a point. As the unposited point is at once everywhere and nowhere, so are these activities everywhere and nowhere They are what is expressed by the Sanscrit words Purusha and Prakriti, the unmanifested principles of soul and matter or form, of energy and causation, of the impulse of desire and the condition of its fruition Mr. Betts calls them the ideal activities of Positing and Determining They are unmanifested principles, but of their union comes all manifestation.

From the first law that " Being shall exist " Mr. Betts deduces the corollary " Being exists in variety." If Infinite Being is to be manifested in finite existence it must be through infinite variation of the finite, for otherwise the cosmos would be a manifestation of monotony, not of infinity.

In other words, Maya, to use a Sanscrit term again, is the eternal form of manifestation. Nothing is permanent in the universe, save impermanence—change. Only the abstract duality—the polar aspects of the one substance, the infinite Alpha and Omega, which is the source of all things, and in which all things live, and move, and have their being—endures unchanged. Under whatsoever changing forms it may appear, duality, polarity, antithesis, is the one unchanging law of evolution

SECTION IV.

PRINCIPLES OF REPRESENTATION.

WHEN we contemplate our consciousness—and in the fact that *we* can contemplate consciousness as *ours*, lies a proof of the duality of the self which will presently be brought to light in the diagrams—when we contemplate our consciousness we find there one element which differs from all the rest. Whereas *they* are multitudinous, chaotic, changing, *it* is one, alone, comparatively unchanged. It may be called the undifferentiable differentiation of the One, and all the other elements are related to this substance. We call it "I," the subject of consciousness The multitudinous changing elements we call the objects of consciousness. The relation of object to subject on the lowest plane is sense, on a higher plane intellectual faculty, on the highest knowledge. I see, I think of, I know that I see and think of . . . some object.

The ego, although not discretely different at different times as the objects of consciousness are, is continuously different, at least the phenomenal ego is constantly moving, though the noumenon is unchanged. The ego of manhood feels itself to be different from what it was during childhood or youth; consequently the true representation of the ego would be an actual point constantly shifting its position, moving in an orbit; but for convenience of representation it is necessary to represent the actual point as fixed, the centre of each diagram; and besides, it is only by reasoning that we become conscious of the changing nature of our ego just as by reasoning we discover the motion of the earth. We feel as if our centre were fixed, and so far as its relation to its own activities are concerned it is fixed   The ego is always the centre of the diagram wherever the diagram may be located.

From this central point of consciousness, the ego, proceeds a circuit of ideal activity which is its endowment of life-energy in the abstract—the particular share of the lesser a (alpha) in the infinite circuit of the great A (alpha). This life-energy constitutes the possibility of the individual life. It is impulse, desire, tendency of the ego to go out of itself. It has no absolute limit save that the ego is within the ideal circumference of Prakriti. That is to say Existence itself is limited by the abstract ideas of Time and

B

Space—the ego is dependent upon causation, condition, for the fruition of its desires. → human desire.

Since Mr. Betts is studying, not the evolution of a universe, but the evolution of man, he begins, instead of with the first great cause, with the proximate determining cause.

Each determining cause conditions a definite expression of consciousness, a sensation, in the circuit of unconscious life-energy which is the basis of consciousness. The circuit is indicated in the diagrams by outgoing and incoming arrows. The amount of activity thus determined assumes a definite condition

The first sensation produced by the action of a determining cause is simple consciousness, the feeling of being alive   To this succeed touch, sight, hearing, taste, and smell ; and on the hypothesis of the Septenary law of perfectness there must still remain the possibility of two latent senses not yet determined.

Every sensation alternates with a pause or blank of non-sensation, the ebb from the state of consciousness to the state of unconsciousness again. This agrees with Francis Galton's theory of the pulsatory character of attention

All activity whose condition is determined or differentiated Mr. Betts calls " real" activity, and he represents it in the diagrams by an ordinary line. Undifferentiated, unconscious energy he calls " ideal" activity, and represents it by a dotted line.

It will be observed that Mr. Betts uses the word " real" in a different sense from that in which " reality" is regarded as synonymous with " truth," the inner reality. In the present instance it connotes first apparent reality, that which has to do with the things and affairs of sense, the nominalism of the schoolmen. Such application is not inconsistent with the derivation of the word "real"—*i e ,* belonging to things. Reality or realisation felt first in connection with external things, appearances, is gradually perceived more and more interiorly as consciousness developes through succeeding stages, until finally Truth is perceived as the only reality.

At first sight it may appear as though the determining agent were something wholly foreign to the individual entity, but a little consideration must convince us that causation is as much a necessary element in the evolution of an existence as the possession of the life-energy itself. Without a complementary objective activity, to complete the subjective activity, existence must be merely potential, not actual. Mr. Betts plainly perceived that all proximate determinants are but the links in the chain of causation, whose root is the law that " Being exists in variety."

Causation acts, as was shown, as a determinant on the manifestation of the undifferentiated energy. For a determinant to have any effect at all it must be within certain limits of proportion to the activity determined, otherwise no result will arise, interaction being impossible.

Every conditioning agent, whatever may be its plane of operation, in its ultimate analysis is resolvable into pulsation, vibration. For instance, vibrations within definite limits of velocity cause a determination of consciousness as sensations of Light and Colour, other vibrations having a slower rate, sensations of sound, and so for the other senses, in accordance with the law of determination. It is not inconceivable that beings might exist to whose internal activity the external vibrations we call Light and Sound might appear differently, so that the determinant that produces the sensation of sight in us might excite the sense of hearing in them ; thus sight would be indeed the " music of the spheres," or with a changed relation again, sound might be visible, as Coleridge pictures in his beautiful fragment of " Kubla Khan"—

> .   .   .   " With music loud and long,
> I would build that dome in air,
> That sunny dome ! those caves of ice !
> And all who heard should see them there "

Or there might be beings of ampler development yet who could adjust any sense to any series of vibrations, tuning their instruments, so to speak, to the required pitch.

If the optic nerve could be related to some force akin to Electricity instead of Light an immense expansion of the power of vision would accrue, for in Electricity a long line of action takes the place of a point of radiation. Distance would be practically annihilated, as we should be able to receive almost instantaneous optic telegrams of the most distant scenes. Some adjustment of this nature may be the explanation of the phenomena of clairvoyance and other of those mysterious inner senses, whose existence in no small number of persons it is hardly possible to doubt in face of the constantly increasing mass of affirmative evidence.

We know through their chemical effects that there

are rays of light vibrating more rapidly than the violet rays, which cause us no answering sensation of colour Possibly in the process of evolution, as our determining law enlarges, we may develope the consciousness of new and unknown colours beyond the violet or below the red rays.

rainbow Colours.

It is a curious survival of a fragment of ancient occultism in modern science that we should resort to the expedient of splitting the colour blue into two, blue and indigo, which are nothing but pale and dark blue, in order to preserve the mystic number seven, when really we can see only six colours in the spectrum.

7 outfits.

The action of the determining agent upon the ego is twofold. It causes the realisation of a subjective sensation and of an objective perception. Thus far existence is but a vibratory line, a string of individual isolated instants of consciousness Such probably is the form of the consciousness of a young infant or of a total idiot; a one-dimensional consciousness, the warp of time is being spun, but not the woof woven with it.

After the repeated recurrence of any sensation, though slightly varying in form, the individual developes the consciousness of its identity, and he begins to form an image or idea, both of the subjective sensation and of the accompanying objective perception, which he can retain in his mind though the sense affection of which it is the counterpart is transitory. Mr. Betts calls this power of ideation Imagination, using it in the literal sense of the word. As a prism receives a beam of light and deflects the rays, holding them apart so that the colours of the spectrum are separated and distinguished, so Imagination receives the stream of Consciousness, and holds apart and compares the different experiences.

Comparison is represented in the diagrams by the angle; Consciousness from one-dimensional becomes two-dimensional, the line is expanded to a surface.

Let us suppose a state of consciousness in which but two senses are developed—sight and touch—and that a sensation of touch is being perceived at the present moment. This being a conscious state is diametrically opposed to the previous unconscious state. The unconscious state was represented by a dotted line, or rather circuit, of undetermined length proceeding from the central point, the ego. The conscious state is represented by an actual line of limited length, and this line also is polar, subjective sensation proceeding from the centre outwards, and sense perception from the outer end of the line inwards. The other kind of sensation which has been realised, that of sight, which at the present moment exists only as an idea, being opposed both to the existing conscious and the alternate unconscious state, is represented by a line at right angles to each. And since every idea is dual— e.g., the positive idea of light brings with it the negative complementary idea of darkness—of a colour, its complementary colour—therefore the positive representative line on the right hand of the diagram is duplicated by a counterpart line on the left. The sensation of the present moment is not yet reflected as an idea, nor distinguished by comparison. In the diagram it is the apex of the form. When more than two senses occupy Consciousness the lines representing them are arranged radially round the centre. Although the distinction must then be represented by a smaller angle, it does not follow that it is less in amount, as the form itself of Consciousness has become enlarged. At the same time it is quite possible that when the number of modes of manifestation is very limited the sensations are more vivid, and consequently the distinctions more marked, than when more modes of consciousness are differentiated.

When studying the race rather than the individual the apex of the Onden would symbolise the sense whose evolution is proceeding with the greatest activity at any given period—the sense whose sensations are the most desired and which is becoming the most delicately discriminative. At the present time this seems to be the sense of taste.

Imagination, according to Mr. Betts, is a polar activity. Besides its positive function of comparison whereby ideas are held apart and distinguished, it has also the negative function of combining them into a unity, so that we feel the continuity of Consciousness to be unbroken. This is represented in the diagrams by the contour, the outer boundary, of the figure. Mr. Betts calls this the line of Memory, but the line of Experience would be a better designation, since by Memory he means the recording activity, because Experience is the resultant of forgotten as well as remembered facts of sensation and perception. The various lines of differentiated activity, the radii, are united in the central point, the ego, out of which they originate; being related to the ego as being *its* activities, and therefore one, and separated at their circumferential ends, in which they are themselves, distinct and manifold. They are recombined by the contour, the line of experience, as being comprised within the consciousness of the particular entity. The same union, separation, and recombination takes place for the negative as well as for the positive lines of ideation. They may be compared to the positive and negative spectra of polarised light.

We have now, first, the *Abstract Consciousness*, or bare ego, which is ideal, unmanifested, represented by a dotted circuit; next we have the consciousness of *Sensation*, or the ego manifested as its own object— *e.g.*, I see, represented by an ordinary line from the centre, the ego, outwards; and immediately following or rather accompanying Sensation we have *objective Perception*, the consciousness of a not-I—I see . . . an object. Perception is represented by the reverse of the line of sensation, for a line AB cannot be drawn without its polar opposite the line BA becoming determined. Then follows the after consciousness of *Imagination* I form an idea which combines my seeing and the object and I distinguish it from other ideas by Comparison. The formation of an idea is represented by the reflection of the line in a new direction, and the Comparison of it with previous ideas is represented by the angle through which it is turned. The combining of this idea with previous ideas in the unity of the experience of life is represented by the boundary line of the figure. There is yet one other step of the sense-consciousness to be represented. The idea which has been present in consciousness dies down into a latent or unconscious state; the attention is withdrawn from it and directed to something else. The idea is not gone from the consciousness entirely, for the image of the idea I have formed remains with me in a latent state. I can direct my attention to it again, and recognise it, consequently this state is sometimes called the causal state, since it can cause the idea to be realised again and again. This is represented by the dotted obverse form in the diagrams It is dotted because it is an ideal state, not realised, only dimly felt. In it the causal image of everything that *has been* realised in the consciousness is contained, as in the original circuit of ideal activity every idea that *can be* realised in the consciousness is potentially contained.

The causal consciousness is felt as a permanent substratum or substance of Thought which vibrates between its realised forms and the formless causal idea The causal form is the realisation subjectively, for we cannot realise it objectively, of the ideal activity itself which is the very substance of life. As the obverse of Sensation it is the realisation of the substance of life, and as the obverse of Perception it gives permanence to the world of objects by giving a reflex feeling of substance to these also; whence arises our conception of matter as the changeless substance of the objective forms we perceive. The idea of Matter, like that of Life, can only be subjectively, not objectively, realised. We have no sensuous perception of matter, we infer it from the persistence of our ever-changing impressions of objects of sense.

SECTION V.

THE POLAR-OPPOSITE FORMS AND THE MEAN FORM OF SENSE-CONSCIOUSNESS. THE OND, ONDE, AND ONDEN FIGURES

THE figures numbered 1, 2, 3, represent the animal sense-consciousness which underlies the human or rational sense-consciousness. Mr. Betts calls it the neutral or undetermined form, and distinguishes it by the name of the Onden (*Unda*). The figures 4, 5, 6, 7, Mr. Betts calls indifferently positive, or male or alpha form of human sense-consciousness, and figures 8, 9, 10, 11, which are the counterparts of these, the negative or female or omega forms. The alpha form he names the Ond, the omega form the Onde. The terms, Ond and Onde, denote the genera; they include endless specific variations of form according to the varying proportion of the polar activities, whence they are evolved. This variation is represented by the introduction of a numerical scale for dividing the lines of perception and angles of imagination In the Onden a scale is used, having a series of equal terms, as 1, 1, 1, 1, etc., for the measurement of the successive limitations of consciousness. For the Ond, any scale having a constantly increasing ratio of progression is used, as 1, 2, 3, 4. For the Onde the scale is reversed, being applied in the opposite direction. The fact of the scale having increasing terms, instead of equal terms, marks the distinction between the purely animal and the rational sense, the amount of intensity in the scale of progression denoting the degree of rationality attained—*e g.*, if 1, 1, 1, 1, 1, etc , represent animal consciousness, 1, 1 1, 1·2, 1·3, 1·4, etc., might be taken to represent the order of consciousness of a very low savage—perhaps some bushman or cave-dweller but little removed from the brutes— 1, 1·5, 2, 2·5, 3, 3·5, etc., would represent a more advanced consciousness, perhaps that of a member of a pastoral race or an agricultural one, 1, 2, 3, 4, 5, 6, would represent still higher intelligence, and so on, up to the rational consciousness of a highly civilised man, yet one whose purpose of life is still on the sensuous plane.

It would seem as if in the Onden the number of terms in the scale should be limited to five, the five senses we have, or at any rate to seven, if the hypothesis of Septenary completeness be adopted. Mr. Betts has not so limited them. He forms Ondens with scales having any given number of equal terms. Perhaps he does not regard the number of possible senses as limited, but conceives that in different worlds, or different world periods, man may be evolved from a broader or narrower basis of animalism. There is an ancient Persian legend which represents man as having been created first a quadruped—a horse-man or centaur—but, falling short of his high destiny, he was destroyed, and man the biped, male and female, succeeded him.

In the rational consciousness the differentiated activities must be regarded rather as faculties derived through sense—*e g.*, speech and music through hearing, than as the senses themselves.

Apparently an animal experiences an equally vivid enjoyment in the exercise of any of its faculties, but man discriminates between his different desires according to some ratio of proportion.

Numbers are discontinuous A numerical scale of acceleration expresses the relations of discontinuous terms. A line is continuous, and hence may be taken as the representation of a continuously increasing activity or motion, but the ratio of acceleration will not be manifest unless the line is broken up into discontinuous portions.

At every moment the temporary limit of possible consciousness, the outermost circle in the Ond diagram, is being extended further within the eternally-limiting circumference of Prakriti (which might be represented by a dotted circle enclosing each diagram); and each smaller circle, each mode of sense-consciousness, is expanding simultaneously with the whole: both their area becomes greater and their distinctions more marked (*i.e.*, the terms of the scale have an increased ratio of proportion).

Within these expanding circles of possibility the actual form of the consciousness, the realised experience of the ego expands. From time to time some new mode of consciousness, some new faculty, is differentiated—*i.e.*, a new circle is added to the diagram, a new term to the numerical scale, according to which it is evolved. Thus progress is both continuous and discontinuous; continuous progress in discrete forms: the line divided by application of number to it.

The interaction of the positive activity of the ego,

and the negative activity of the determinant, produces the consciousness of objective reality. Each several cognition by the ego of the non-ego as an object of consciousness adds some accretion to the entire quantity of consciousness realised. It is so much won from the domain of the ideal to that of the real, from the abstract to the concrete.

Such interaction is followed by a reaction in which the poles of the activities are reversed. That of the determinant becoming positive, and that of the ego passive. Objects have an emotional effect upon the ego which it cognises and compares, taking stock of its emotions and relating them to itself as modifications of the quality of its existence. Thus subjective intension is added to objective extension of consciousness.

This progressive qualification of consciousness is represented by the Onde, as the progressive quantification of consciousness is by the Ond. The latter starts from a centre of possibility and extends itself *ad infinitum* into objectivity. The former starts from an objective circumference absolutely limited for the time being, and qualifies itself subjectively *ad infinitum*. Thus a complementary form of consciousness is evolved, a form contingent on the evolution of the first form. The Ond may be called the form of the Intellect, and the Onde the form of the Emotion of a rational ego on the sense plane.

Mutatis mutandis, the Ond and Onde may be regarded as representatives of various other antithetical counterparts which are in correspondence with these— *e.g.,* of man and woman, for although man and woman considered independently are alike, each having intellectual and emotional consciousness, yet, considered in their relations to each other, man is the active form, the originator, and woman the receptive or passive form, the moulder of human existence.

In the Onde the activities are measured by the scale in the reverse direction to those of the Ond, viz., from circumference to centre in progressive ratio of acceleration instead of from centre to circumference.

The Onden can be formed in either way, and by whichever method it is formed, and whatever the number of terms in the scale used, the contour of the form is always the same, a neutral form—the androgene from which sex is evolved.

The apex of the Ond is less than a right angle, and as more and more terms are added to the scale and as the ratio of acceleration is augmented, the angle becomes less and less until the form is scarcely distinguishable from a straight line. Were it possible to determine the Ond to infinity it would be resolved into a straight line, which may therefore be regarded as the ideal type or limit of intellectual operation.

Conversely the Ond has an apex greater than a right angle, and in proportion to the increase of the terms of the scale and the increase of their ratio, the angle becomes greater and greater and the form tends more and more to become circular. Determined to infinity the Onde would be resolved into a circle, the ideal type of emotion.

The Onden is the equilibrium between the opposite poles, the mean form between the straight line and the circle.

The dotted obverse or causal form is also neutral or undetermined as to polar quality. For Ond and Onde it is the same, and varies scarcely at all with the varying scales.

SECTION VI.

THE THREE KINDS OF NUMERICAL PROGRESSION, ARITH-METICAL, GEOMETRICAL, AND HARMONICAL, AND THEIR EQUIVALENT IN CONSCIOUSNESS.

FURTHER EXPLANATION OF THE MECHANICAL WORKING OF THE DIAGRAMS.

AT the side of each diagram there is a formula which is the key to explain of what kind the figure is, viz., Ond, Onde or Onden, and what are the scales used in developing it. The Greek capital letter A or Ω or the letter U denotes that the form is an Ond, an Onde, or an Onden. A indicates positive or male, Ω, negative or female, and U, neutral or un-determined as to kind. On the right-hand side of the Greek symbol is a letter of the English alphabet— F or J or H or some other. This letter denotes the number of terms in the scale used. F stands for six, being the sixth letter in the alphabet, H for eight, and so on. Beneath the Greek symbol is a letter denoting the kind of progression used—viz., Arithmetical, Geo-metrical, or Harmonical, A, G, or H. A1 denotes arithmetical progression, common difference 1.—$i\,e.$, 1, 2, 3, &c. A·1 arithmetical progression, common difference ·1—$i.e.$, 1, 1·1, 1·2, &c. For Geometrical progression the multiple 2 is to be understood unless otherwise specified, as G × 3   The Harmonical scale Mr. Betts generally employs is $\frac{1}{8}, \frac{1}{7}, \frac{1}{6}, \frac{1}{5}, \frac{1}{4}, \frac{1}{3}, \frac{1}{2}, 1$.

Multiplicity and similarity are the characteristics of the forms governed by the arithmetical progression. By simply varying the number of terms and the common difference an immense number of forms may be produced differing only by almost imperceptible degrees one from another.   Intense energy characterises the forms governed by geometrical ratios. The superficies of the form is almost swept away by the rush of the impetus to Action.   But few such forms can be generated, since if a large number of terms be taken or if a larger multiple than two be used the form of the Ond becomes practically undistinguishable from a straight line.   The converse is true for the Onde: the emotional element is so developed as to realise almost the whole possibility of Passion, and the form becomes undistinguishable from a circle. The Harmonical forms strike the mean between these two extremes.   Beauty of proportion and harmonious balance are their endowment

These three kinds of progression represent three main lines of human differentiation, which may be called the Mechanical, the Teleological, and the Hedonic. They are not separated one from another by any hard and fast boundary, rather their limits overlap, so to speak, and they run by gradation into one another. The Arithmetical or Mechanical class comprise the ordinary people, the multitude—people whose lives are superficial and their energy diffused.   Like the animals, they are very much the creatures of circumstance and have but little definite purpose or deep feeling. The Geometrical or Teleological class comprises the few exceptional people, the leaders, men of strong purpose and deliberate intent. The superficies of life in them is narrowed, but its intensity is immensely increased. The Harmonical or Hedonic class is more numerous than the Teleological but less numerous than the Mechanical. It comprises the poet, the artist, the prudent statesman, all in whom the æsthetic element predominates. As typical of national rather than of individual forms the Arithmetical diagrams would represent Democracy, the Geometrical Autocracy, and the Harmonical well-organised Republics or Constitutional Monarchies.

It is not, Mr. Betts asserts, so much the looking at the completed diagrams as the actual working of them out according to their law that will enable us to perceive their correspondence with the forms of human consciousness. Lest any difficulty should be experienced in working out the diagrams some further explanation of the mechanical construction is perhaps desirable before proceeding further with the metaphysical interpretation

For figure 1, symbolised as U, therefore an Onden, a scale of six terms (F) is used—*i.e*, 1, 1, 1, 1, 1, 1 The line of perception is divided into six equal parts. Circles of possible ideation are described through each division of the line. For the measurement of the angles of comparison the same scale is used, and in order to facilitate the angular measurement each term of the scale is computed from zero 1, 2, 3, 4, 5, 6; the entire scale is then taken as the unit, and the

terms are reduced to decimal fractions; thus the
scale for the angular measurement becomes as near
as may be   ·166
                    ·333
                    ·500
                    ·660
                   1 000

These spaces can easily be measured off by means of
a circular protractor,* with the semicircles decimally
divided, which Mr. Betts has made for the purpose,
in which the semicircle being equivalent to 1 000,
each large division represents ·100 and each small
division ·010. Subdivisions can be guessed with
sufficient correctness. The positive radii are measured
off to the right and the negatives to the left from
zero. A considerable number of scales reduced to
decimals in this manner are subjoined. They are
only approximately correct, as it is inconvenient to
make use of more than three places of decimals.
For perfect accuracy the diagrams would have to be
made of a very large size

The line of perception is really a congeries of lines,
since each realised activity proceeds out of the central
point, and through the former circles of differentiation.
Each new faculty developed is, in a sense, inclusive
of the former ones. The several lines of perception,
limited according to the scale of progression, are
turned aside to the right and left and separated by
angles proportionate to the scale of progression. The

---

* A protractor printed on cardboard accompanies each copy
of this work. It should be cut out and the small circle cut from
the centre before using it.

contour is drawn from the centre through the farthest end points of these lines, right and left to the apex of the figure

Figure 2 is exactly the same as figure 1, but measured by ĸ, *i.e.*, by a scale of ten terms. ɪ and ᴊ are counted as one. Figure 3 is a repetition of figure 2, but with the addition of the obverse form. For practical convenience in constructing the forms Mr. Betts usually produces the lines of reflection to the outer circumference, and then the contour is drawn through the successive points of intersection of the first line and first circle, second line and second circle, and so on; and the obverse dotted form is similarly drawn, but in the opposite direction.

· The Ond, figure 4, is drawn in a precisely similar manner, except that a scale having proportionate terms instead of equal terms is used. It is the scale of ʜ—*i.e.*, it has eight terms—in kind it is A 1—*i e*, arithmetical progression common difference 1 *i e* 1, 2, 3, 4, 5, 6, 7, 8, or, reckoning each term from zero, 1, 3, 6, 10, 15, 21, 28, 36. The decimal scale for the angles will be found in the list of scales under the heading A 1, ʜ. The scales are applied in exactly the same way as the Onden scales.

The Ond, figure 5, is also in a scale of eight terms of Arithmetical progression, but with common difference ·1 —hence it is but little removed in form from the Onden. The Ond figure 6 is in a scale of eight terms of Harmonical progression; H, ʜ, in the list of decimal scales. The Ond, figure 7, is in a scale of eight terms of Geometrical progression, G, ʜ, in the list. Any other scales may be selected, and an endless

variety of diagrams produced having the same construction as these.

The Onde, figure 8, has the same scale as the Ond,
figure 4   The line of perception is divided by scale
from the circumferential point to the central point
The circles of emotional possibility are drawn through
each division, and the realised emotions, the limited
lines, are reflected right and left and separated by
angles proportionate to the scale used.   The contour is
drawn from the apex of the form to the centre,
right and left; and the dotted contour of the obverse
form is drawn in the opposite direction.   The Onde,
figure 9, has the same scale as the Ond, figure 5;
it also rather resembles an Onden, having a very low
order of scale.   The Onde, figure 10, has the same
scale as the Ond, figure 6; and the Onde, figure 11,
the same scale as the Ond, figure 7.   As all these
are constructed on precisely the same principle no
detailed explanation is necessary.   In the Onde,
figure 11, the outer circles have to be so close together
that they are scarcely distinguishable.   In the Ond,
figure 7, two circles have had to be omitted round
the centre, as they are too small to be engraved.
They must be imagined within the innermost circle
that is represented.

SECTION VII

VARIATION.

In the examples of consciousness which have been given the various undulations of real activity into which the original simple circuit of the ideal activity has been differentiated flow on in a complex rhythm of harmony. There is no impulse left undetermined, no want left unsatisfied, and thus no incentive to further progress, seeing that completeness is already attained, though but of a low order. It is the discord, the conflict of opposites—power struggling with condition, and yearning seeking satisfaction that impel men on towards the realisation of a higher plane of existence than consists in personal gratification and the enjoyment of externals

The original Alpha and Omega forms in their simple perfectness may be taken as the representation of Adam and Eve in the earthly Paradise—types which are approximately realised in the early youth of every man or every race born under favourable circumstances. The simple savage living amid bountiful Nature feels little or no disproportion between his desires and their fruition. His wants are so few and simple that he can easily gratify them, and the means of gratification are at hand It is true there must be from the first some lurking dissatisfaction with every realisation of the ideal, since no realisation can exhaust the ideal; and had it been otherwise there could have been no progress But at first the dissatisfaction is so unrealised that it does not force itself upon the attention. It lies latent in the consciousness, and hence is not represented in the diagrams But the perfect type must be broken through, the serpent of dissatisfaction must bring discord into Eden that ultimately a higher perfectness than ignorant innocence may be realised, that of purity which, knowing good and evil, freely chooses good.

Since Being must exist and can only be manifested in the finite through infinite variation, there must necessarily be in every man some disproportion between his alpha and omega activities, whether of perception or imagination. This disproportion at first leads a man on unconsciously, as he thinks to experience yet greater delight with each new fruition of desire. But as his desires expand, and their gratification is increasingly difficult, the disproportion becomes a conscious element in his existence. A thrill of unsatisfaction accompanies every determination of activity, even the most pleasurable, impelling to the continued search in new directions for new and more perfect means of self-gratification, only to be proved in their turn equally unsatisfying.

"To make one shoeblack happy . . would require, if you consider it," says Carlyle, "for his permanent satisfaction and saturation, simply this allotment, no more and no less—*God's infinite universe altogether to himself*, therein to enjoy infinitely, and fill every wish as fast as it rose . always there is a black spot in the sunshine; it is even, as I said, *the shadow of ourselves.*"

Imperfect determination causes a hiatus to be felt

which acts as a determinant of consciousness into self-consciousness. The child or the simple savage is self-conscious in that his experiences have relation to himself The realisation of imperfection causes a further development of self-consciousness in that he now contemplates his experiences as being *his own.*

A few variations of form arising out of imperfect determination are given in figures 12 to 19. Mr. Betts has not been careful to explain the equivalent in consciousness of each variation in detail. He appears to have done with his wave-forms what Mrs. Boole, the widow of the mathematician, says in her little book on "Symbolic Methods," is possible with any true symbols; having generated them he has let them carry him away, believing that if he worked out the geometrical development, they could at any time be translated into the corresponding terms of life. But there is always a fear in such a case lest, through some flaw in the symbolisation, we should be landed, when we attempt the interpretation, in "Quod est absurdum." Even when further explanation is asked for, Mr. Betts does not seem able to give it in a clear and complete manner; still it is quite possible that he may himself perceive the truth of his representative forms without being able to communicate that perception to others. As James Hinton remarks, "Of all the expounders of a great discovery it is well known that the discoverer himself is one of the worst"

The figures 12 and 13, 14 and 15, 16 and 17, are examples of variation of the Imaginative power. The four former diagrams representing a deficient, and the two latter an excessive development of Imagination, as

referred to the normal standard Deficiency occasions a
narrowing of the form, which represents a meagreness
of the ideas, a barrenness of the images produced in the
consciousness. Excess occasions a spiral overlapping of
the contour of the form : the power of perception of
new ideas is overbalanced by the tendency to redun-
dant diffuseness, producing a shallow superficiality
of character.

In the former diagrams the positive ideas and their
negative counterparts occupied respectively one-half
of the circle of comparison The semi-circle may
therefore be taken as the standard of a normal imagination. The activity of Imagination is formularised
as ϕ This symbol is placed by the side of the letters
denoting the scale used. $\phi 5$ denotes that half, $\phi \cdot 33$
that one-third, and $\phi 2$ that double the semi-circle is
occupied by positive and negative radii respectively, in
the last case the positive reflections of activities are
arranged radially round the entire circle in one direction, and the negative radii in the other, producing
an overlapping of the sides of the figure.

The next class of forms, those represented in figures
18 and 19, 20 and 21, 22 and 23, show the really vital
variation of consciousness. They are the fall which
renders possible a higher perfectness—the discord
which may lead up from melody to harmony. In
these forms there is an element of necessary undeterminateness in the very nature of the consciousness Instead of being governed by a simple law
it has a complex law which is represented by the
combination of two or more different scales of progression—for instance, one might take the harmonical

scale of J and the arithmetical scale of G—the relation between the two scales would produce a conflict which would affect the entire existence—the man now rising to his higher possibilities and then again sinking to his lower level   The form cannot be fully determined, either by J or G, but must determine itself as it can in a compromise between the two   The ego appears free to determine itself as it chooses between these two laws, but that is only because the law which governs the choice is not brought to light on this ground. On a higher plane this apparent freewill is included in the necessity imposed by the law of development, and a new element of apparent freedom takes its place. To take a concrete example of the compound scale of development on the lower ground, one may imagine a man whose highest possibilities might find expression as a poet, but whose lower tendencies would lead him perhaps to commerce   His life might be a continual conflict between his poetic aspirations and his greed of gain, now one and now the other having predominance, causing halts and breaks in the experience, such are represented by the indentations in the contour.

The compound scale is the equivalent of the bias of the nature, certain impulses being strong out of due proportion to the rest. The limitation which prevents the higher possibilities from being fully realised produces the consciousness of sin and shortcoming, yet this very limitation is the foundation of the individuality and idiosyncracy of character which on a higher plane render social union and corporate unity possible. But although the Ond contains the germs for future development no true brotherhood is possible, while the form remains enchained within the circle of self-gratification. It does but oscillate in unstable equilibrium between its conflicting desires. These imperfect forms, their author remarks, resemble Algebraic Surds, quantities that can never be perfectly rationalised and their root found, except, perhaps, through association with other quantities, which also may possibly present an equally insoluble problem when taken separately.

It has been stated that every positive conception involves a negative counterpart; thus it would appear as if the two sides of every figure, though reversed, should be in other respects similar, but in the diagrams under consideration it is not so. The explanation of this appears to be that, although when any idea is realised the complementary idea must be latent in the consciousness, it may be that no attention is paid to it; it is not necessarily realised either equally or simultaneously with the other. Sometimes a negative conception is realised more vividly and earlier in point of time than a positive conception. One may often observe people in whom there exists a very strong sense of injustice, while it is impossible to make them perceive the opposite idea of justice, though certainly this idea is involved in the other.

In some of the diagrams the negatives are governed by a higher scale than the positives. Possibly this may be intended to represent a pessimistic, and the reverse an optimistic, disposition. The negative as well as the positive attributes may be governed by compound scales. In the negative as well as the positive realisation, indentations appear in the line of experience as the form oscillates between its two laws. The breaks caused by the oscillation resemble the cusps in the curves of leaves. Where the breaks occur is decided arbitrarily on this first ground. Their position cannot be determined by geometrical method until the law governing them becomes manifest on a higher ground.

The undeterminateness of the actual form of consciousness reacts upon the obverse form, causing a shadow of power undefined and want unsatisfied to hover round it, mingling with the feeling of life a haunting dread of Death and Destruction.

Further variations arise out of the growing complexity of the law of determination as the evolution proceeds, for activity can be determined by negative as well as positive determinants. What we have realised but *have not* exercises as real an effect on consciousness as what we *have*. An activity that has been conditioned as Love, by means of a determinant, some object of love, might be absolutely limited in that particular direction, and determined into its polar opposite, hate. Mr Betts has not drawn any examples of such variations arising out of the law of determination among the plane forms, but on the higher ground the forms of the bi-axial corollas contain a somewhat similar principle of reaction through absolute limitation.

Any or all classes of variation may be combined in the same form. We can have scales differing in kind, or in degree, or in both, for the positive and negative attributes; also we may have a combination of different scales for each of these; besides this there may be variations of the imaginative power, and variations of the contour. The last class are formularised as χ; Mr. Betts has reserved these also for the diagrams of the third standing-ground.

So far from finding satisfaction in the increasing complexity of the rhythm of life the chasm widens, and the struggle intensifies as the consciousness advances in the long, long path of acquiring the knowledge of good and evil :—

" Ye are nobly born, your Sire is Wisdom, and Love is his wife,
  Who lifted you like a mist from the uttermost bowels of life,
  And moulded a plastic form where ye learnt the firstness of
    things,
  As away from the nestling dream ye were banished to find
    your wings
  Fret and confusion and sorrow, struggle and anger and fight,
  Yea, the form of man's life is as seas that rave in the darkness
    of night;
  Fear and deadness and doubt in the outermost borders from me,
  Yet his birthright's place is my heart, and his glory to come
    back free "

The mechanical construction of the diagrams representing variation requires but little further explanation.

The Ond, figure 12, is in a scale of eight terms of arithmetical progression, common difference ·5. The angular expansion is taken as $\phi\,5$, or one-half the normal, consequently for the angular measurement the scale as given in the list must be divided by 2, and similarly for the Onde, figure 13

The Ond and Onde, figures 14 and 15, have the same scale, but with $\phi\,·33$, or one-third the normal, consequently the angular scale must be divided by 3

The Ond and Onde, figures 16 and 17, have the same scale, but with ϕ 2, or double the normal, therefore the scale for the angular measurement must be multiplied by 2.

The diagrams, figures 18 to 23, although they represent a most important step in the spiritual evolution, are not satisfactory from a mathematical point of view, because Mr Betts has hitherto been unable to discover a law by which to determine where the breaks in the contour, making the cusps of the leaf, would occur. From a metaphysical point of view it is quite correct that their position should be determined arbitrarily because they represent freewill on this ground, so it is right that what appears chance determination should be introduced, but still there must be a law of chance, a scale of discontinuity which interrupts the more continuous laws and whose intervals may be determined if we take a sufficiently long sequence for the real order to become manifest in the apparent disorder While remaining on the first ground it would be impossible to discover the law by which the element of apparent freewill is regulated, yet, since Mr. Betts asserts that on the higher ground the apparent freedom is absorbed into the law of the form, it might be possible, after reaching the platform of the higher life, to look back and discover what had been the hidden law of the earlier ground. Or it may be that this could not be discovered by studying the individual evolution, but would become apparent as a law of sociology—a law governing the association of individuals—in which case it is right that this element of undeterminateness in the individual should be left unexplained until the laws of the larger evolution are comprehended. The science of sociology is as yet in its infancy, so perhaps it would be premature to expect that we should be able to find the geometrical equivalent for the law determining the position of a unit in a unity, especially as no true social unity is possible on this lowest ground of human evolution. Such personal idiosyncracy as is developed is but the shaping of the bricks for the future building. It would be an interesting application of Mr. Betts's system of geometrical symbology to take some portion of history and represent the periods of progress and decline by curves something similar to those he has used for these representations of individual evolution, and endeavour to determine approximately the relative strength of the opposite forces at work, and by studying a long period to find out the law of the apparently chance element which determines the turning points of a nation towards better or worse.

Perhaps Mr. Betts may yet discover a scientific method of determining the indentations of the contour of his Ond forms, or, if not he, some student of his system may be able to throw further light on the Law of Freewill.

In figure 18, an Ond in arithmetical progression, common difference 1, the right side of the form, the positive ideation, is governed by the scales E G   A compromise is effected between the scale of five terms and that of seven terms   Mr Betts draws five circles of differentiation and seven radii of realised activity arranged according to the scale of comparison.

Thus the realised activity, though equal in amount, is more limited in extent than it would have been if it had been perfectly developed in the scale of G The two circles of differentiation which have been suppressed through the lower necessity would have afforded the perfect realisation of the higher law of the nature. The contour of the experience manifests three stages of progress, one of decline, and three of progress again, $1+1+1-1+1+1+1=7$ It might equally well have been $1+1-1+1+1+1+1=7$—$i\ e.$, any total of seven links, whether ascending or descending The left side of the figure, the negative ideation, is governed by the scales D F in a similar manner. The contour is $1+1+1-1+1+1=6$.

The counterpart form, figure 19, has similar indentations.

The next Ond apparently would represent not possibilities unrealised, but rather an indolent and stupid nature, which hardly perceives what is passing before it, and through inattention misses the experience of life which it might gain. The positive side is determined according to scales of G and E G is now the dominant scale, and governs the circles of differentiation, and E the comparison of the radii, consequently the imagination has allowed the difference between E and G to escape observation. The contour of experience is incomplete, and is not perfectly united with the centre The negative side of the figure is similarly developed, but in scales F and D. The Onde, figure 21, has the same scales as its counterpart. In the Ond, figure 22, the positive side is governed by scales E M, and the negative side by scales D K Consequently the conflict between the higher and the lower possibilities is very marked. The contour of experience has violent ascents and descents, and is far indeed from a full realisation of the scale of M, which would be the ideal perfection of the form on this plane of life   The omega counterpart is similarly determined.

The entire Ond form represents a definite period of conscious existence. If we look back on our life as a whole it will be seen to be divided into various distinct periods or cycles of activity, in each of which consciousness has become somewhat enlarged in character, and the purpose of life has more or less changed its direction. So that, regarding Life as a whole, it may be compared to the whorl of leaves about the stalk of a growing plant, the stalk being the permanent inner life which continues comparatively unchanged amid the changes of the thought. Or, taking a still broader view, the leaves of life, the Onds, may be regarded as the successive incarnations of the ego in the objective world of causes, and the stem of life that supports the whorl of leaves as the alternating periods of subjective life in the world of effects which we call Heaven, or in the Eastern phraseology which has recently become familiarised — *Devachan.*

U_F

U_K

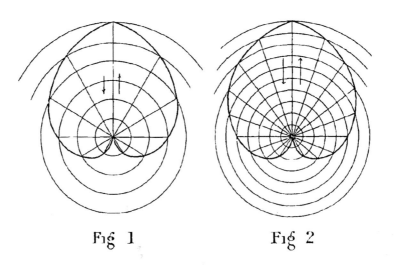

Fig 1   Fig 2

U_K

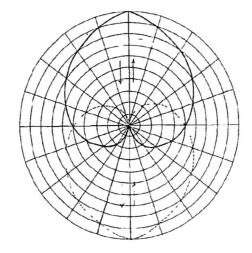

Fig. 3

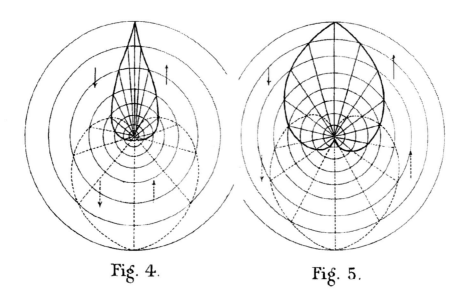

$\dfrac{A_H}{A_1}$ $\dfrac{A_H}{A_1}$

Fig. 4.   Fig. 5.

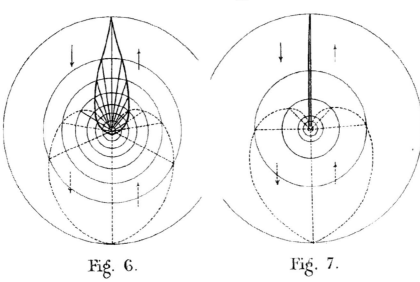

$\dfrac{A_H}{H}$ $\dfrac{A_H}{G}$

Fig. 6.   Fig. 7.

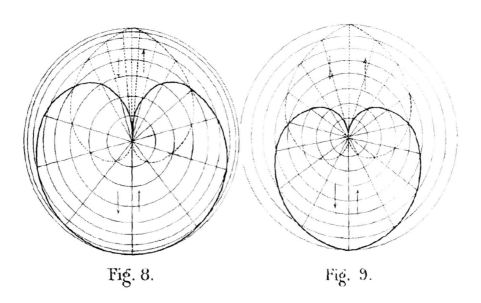

Fig. 8.

Fig. 9.

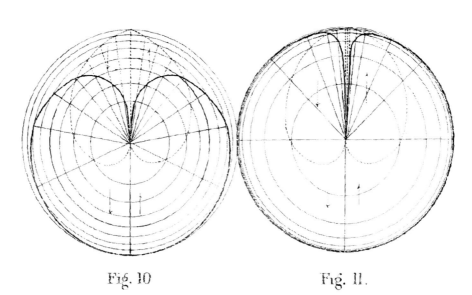

Fig. 10

Fig. 11.

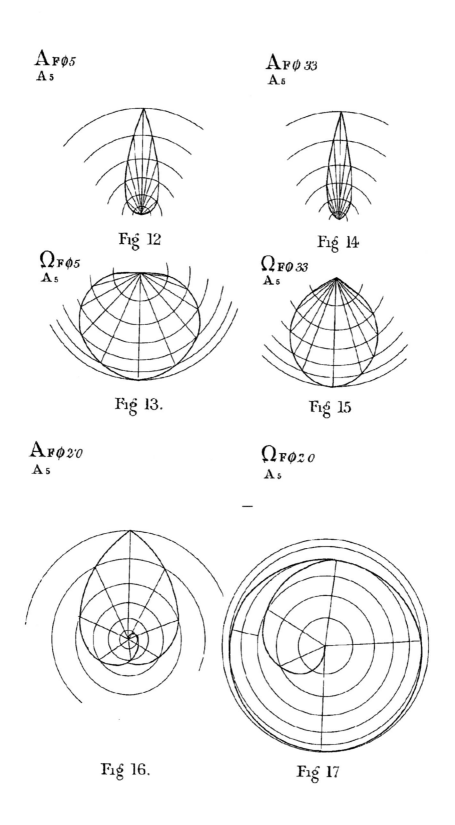

$A_{F\phi 5}$
A_5

Fig 12

$A_{F\phi 33}$
A_5

Fig 14

$\Omega_{F\phi 5}$
A_5

Fig 13.

$\Omega_{F\phi 33}$
A_5

Fig 15

$A_{F\phi 20}$
A_5

$\Omega_{F\phi 20}$
A_5

Fig 16.

Fig 17

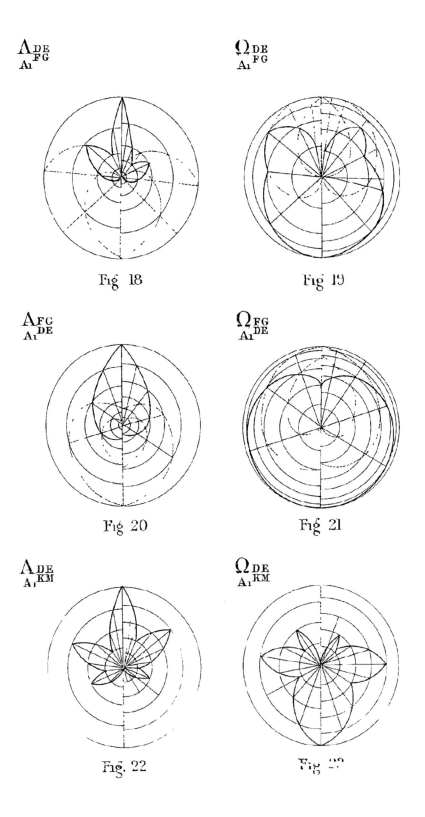

$$\Lambda^{DE}_{A_1 FG}$$

Fig 18

$$\Omega^{DE}_{A_1 FG}$$

Fig 19

$$A^{FG}_{A_1 DE}$$

Fig 20

$$\Omega^{FG}_{A_1 DE}$$

Fig 21

$$\Lambda^{DE}_{A_1 KM}$$

Fig. 22

$$\Omega^{DE}_{A_1 KM}$$

Fig. 23

-

D

SCALES FOR THE ANGULAR MEASUREMENT OF THE DIAGRAMS.

EQUAL TERMS.

A	B	C	D	E	F	G	H	I	K	L	M
1·000	·500	·333	·250	·200	·166	·143	·125	·111	·100	·091	·083
	1·000	·666	·500	·400	·333	·285	·250	·222	·200	·182	·166
		1·000	·750	·600	·500	·428	·375	·333	·300	·272	·249
			1·000	·800	·666	·571	·500	·444	·400	·363	·333
				1·000	·833	·714	·625	·555	·500	·454	·416
					1·000	·857	·750	·666	·600	·545	·500
						1·000	·875	·777	·700	·636	·583
							1·000	·888	·800	·727	·666
								1·000	·900	·818	·750
									1·000	·910	·833
										1·000	·916
											1·000

ARITHMETICAL PROGRESSION—COMMON DIFFERENCE 1.

A	B	C	D	E	F	G	H	I	K	L	M
1·000	·333	·166	·100	·067	·048	0·36	·028	·022	·019	·015	·013
	1·000	·500	·300	·201	·143	·107	·084	·067	·055	·045	·038
		1·000	·600	·401	·286	·214	·167	·134	·109	·090	·077
			1·000	·667	·476	·357	·278	·223	·182	·151	·128
				1·000	·714	·536	·417	·334	·273	·227	·192
					1·000	·750	·584	·467	·382	·318	·269
						1·000	·778	·622	·509	·421	·359
							1·000	·800	·654	·542	·462
								1·000	·818	·682	·577
									1·000	·830	·705
										1·000	·846
											1·000

ARITHMETICAL PROGRESSION—COMMON DIFFERENCE 5.

A	B	C	D	E	F	G	H	I	K	L	M
1·000	·400	·222	·143	·100	·075	·058	·046	·038	·031	·026	·022
	1·000	·556	·365	·250	·186	·144	·115	·094	·077	·065	·055
		1·000	·643	·450	·334	·258	·206	·168	·139	·117	·100
			1·000	·700	·519	·400	·320	·261	·216	·182	·156
				1·000	·741	·572	·456	·372	·308	·260	·223
					1·000	·771	·615	·501	·416	·351	·301
						1·000	·796	·649	·539	·455	·390
							1·000	·815	·677	·572	·490
								1·000	·831	·702	·601
									1·000	·845	·723
										1·000	·856
											1·000

ARITHMETICAL PROGRESSION—COMMON DIFFERENCE ·1.

	A	B	C	D	E	F	G	H	I	K	L	M
A	1·000	·476	·303	·217	·167	·134	113	·093	·080	·069	·060	·054
B		1·000	·640	·456	·350	·281	236	195	168	·144	·127	·113
C			1·000	·717	·550	·441	369	306	264	·226	·200	·177
D				1·000	·767	·615	512	426	363	·316	·279	247
E					1·000	·801	665	556	·475	·413	·364	·322
F						1·000	·828	695	·594	·517	·455	·403
G							1·000	·843	722	·628	·552	·489
H								1·000	·857	·745	·655	580
I									1·000	·869	·764	·677
K										1·000	·879	·779
L											1·000	·887
M												1·000

HARMONICAL PROGRESSION.

	A	B	C	D	E	F	G	H	I	K	L	M
A	1·000	333	·187	·120	·088	·068	055	·046	·039	·034	·030	·028
B		1·000	·458	·280	·197	·150	·119	·098	·083	·072	·063	·057
C			1·000	·520	·341	·252	·196	·159	133	·115	·100	·089
D				1·000	·560	·388	·292	·233	·192	·164	·141	·125
E					1·000	·592	·421	·325	·263	·222	·188	·165
F						1·000	·614	·448	351	292	243	211
G							1·000	·632	·459	·376	·309	265
H								1·000	·646	·489	·392	·329
I									1·000	·660	·503	·410
K										1·000	·668	·517
L											1·000	·678
M												1·000

GEOMETRICAL PROGRESSION—MULTIPLE 2.

	A	B	C	D	E	F	G	H	I	K	L	M
A	1·000	·334	·143	067	·032	·016	·0079	·0039	·0020	·0009	·0005	·0002
B		1·000	·429	·200	·096	·047	·0236	·0117	·0059	·0028	·0014	·0007
C			1·000	467	·225	·112	·0551	·0674	·0135	·0067	·0034	·0017
D				1·000	·484	·240	·1181	·0588	0293	·0146	·0073	·0036
E					1·000	·492	·2441	·1213	·0607	·0303	·0151	·0075
F						1·000	·4950	·2470	·1233	·0615	·0307	·0153
G							1·0000	·4588	·2485	·1241	·0619	·0310
H								1·0000	·4994	·2492	·1245	·0623
I									1·0000	·4995	·2493	·1248
K										1·0000	·4992	·2498
L											1·0000	·4998
M												1·0000

PART II.

SECTION I.

NEGATIVE MORALITY AND ITS MATHEMATICAL EQUIVALENT.

THE second plane or standing-ground of human life being a negative one, a reaction from the first ground of egotism may be passed over briefly, as it is scarcely at all capable of representation by diagram.

The increased strife of conflicting desires as the counterpart forms expand and their law of development becomes ever more complex and contradictory causes the consciousness to become more and more self-conscious until the ego is forced to pause in the pursuit of pleasure and contemplate existence itself.

Just as after the repeated occurrence of sensations the child or savage begins to identify them and compare them one with another, so now after a more or less prolonged experience of life on the first standing-ground the man begins to reflect on his life as a whole and to distinguish its characteristics, except in the case of those persons who remain all their life enchained on the sensuous plane. He compares the reality of his actual life with his ideal, that dim feeling of absolute life that underlies his consciousness and which is his from the fact that the circuit of his life-energy is contained in the circuit of the great

Alpha, the movement of Universal Spirit or Purusha. His perception awakes to the fact of the delusive and ephemeral character of a life spent in the pursuit of pleasure. He sees that, to satisfy his desire of life through the senses, is an insoluble infinite problem. The more his thirst of life grows the more do the satisfying waters flow backward from his lips. A revulsion of feeling sets in, and he withdraws his desires from their wonted channels.

At this crisis some in disgust of life, have committed suicide; others have reduced life to the extremest negation possible short of death. But more commonly the evolution of this ground consists in the circumscription rather than the annihilation of the former activity. The ego, a mere point at first, becomes a focus, its realised activities concentred and repressed, allowed to act only within the circumscribing circle. In the " I will not" of renunciation and self-control morality begins and the existence first becomes a persistent and independent thing, and takes satisfaction in the consciousness of life as life. The mere impulses of volition of the first standing-ground can scarcely be called Will at all, and no morality is possible except as obedience to external law, and no religion is possible except through external revelation, the affirmation of those egos who have attained a higher stage of progress

The degree in which the second ground of life is manifested varies very widely in different persons. Some never get beyond the barren negative morality of this ground—" the eternal nay," Carlyle calls it. Life never becomes anything to them but the giving up of pleasure, they never reach "the eternal yea," but instead of passing through death to life, wrap the grave clothes about them, and remain in the tomb. Others, on the contrary, pass so easily and quickly from an ideal of pleasure to one of duty, and find such happiness in duty, that the renunciation of the lower pleasure is hardly felt at all. Perhaps in such a case the third ground has already been reached in a former incarnation, so that the early steps are rapidly run through again. Self-conquest becomes easier every time the foe is vanquished.

In the latter stage of evolution of the first ground the form was developed from conflicting scales of progression; owing to this some tendencies will be found to be strong out of due proportion to the rest, and will consequently require a greater exercise of Will to control them, so the form of consciousness on the second plane will not be wholly without personal character.

The circumscribing circle, though ideally a true circle, is actually an irregular circumference. Its eccentricity varies in proportion to the discrepancy of the scales which determine the axes. Mr. Betts calls it a trapezoidal ellipse It is unnecessary to give an illustration of so simple a form. It corresponds in plant growth to the transition from the whorl of leaves about the stem to the protective envelope for the future flower.

The motive of life on the second plane is but a kind of inverted egotism. The ego faces itself and admires itself, save only when it disobeys the ascetic law it has imposed upon itself for its own satisfaction. Though self-control lays the foundation of true morality, alone it is but a barren and negative condition, a consciousness of immense powers with but little result, other than the repressing of the ego's own impulses, consequently it is a negation of life that can only last till the internal energy, ever increasing through repression, bursts its self-imposed bonds and surging upwards, lands the ego on the shore of the higher morality.

SECTION II.

THE EVOLUTION OF THE HIGHER MORALITY—PHILANTHROPY OR ALTRUISM. ITS PRINCIPLES OF REPRESENTATION.

THE death-in-life of the second standing-ground cannot last. It is but the stage of transition from a lower life to a higher one, to which sooner or later there must be an uprising; for the second ground contains within itself a principle of progress.

The energy of the ego circumscribed by Will and held in check from its free exercise on the sensuous plain gains strength by reason of the limitation of its activity, until at length it finds a new outlet for its impulses and leaps upward, rejoicing in a new ideal of life.

As the first ideal was *having*, the passion of personal possession, and the second *not-having*, the first imperfect impulse of sacrifice, now the third becomes *doing;* and not pleasure but duty, not self-gratification but work, is made the aim of life. And virtue is no longer the conforming to an external but the obedience to an internal law

The form of the third ground is the resultant of the combined activity of cubical forces arising out of a point which is for convenience regarded as fixed, viz , the personal ego. The new activity, that of soul, ascends upwards, expanding within a circle which is the resultant of the activities of rational sense-perception and imagination, or extension and expansion.

The circuit of the new activity (every activity is polar) depends upon a point above the form which is conceived of as an absolute and infinite non-ego. For not yet does perception awake to the oneness of the soul, the higher ego, with the infinite ' The first life-centre represents the personal ego, the self that separates from the All. The second life-centre represents the divine ego, the true individuality, the self that unites with the All. A new determining law comes into operation to which the personal ego voluntarily subordinates his activity, regarding this law of internal determination as the expression of the Divine will. In some minds it may rather take the form of a vocation to which the life is voluntarily dedicated, or any other form under which the principle of duty and right may be conceived of.

As the desire of the ego required a non-ego, an object, as the condition of its fruition on the lower ground, so the desire of the higher life requires a non-ego for its fulfilment. The determinant in this case

is not objects but other egos   Mankind supplies the
necessary complement through which the ideal activity
of the ego can be manifested   For its personal aspirations to be realised it must carry others up along
with it   Through the needs of humanity the ideal
activity of soul is embodied in a definite form of duty
and use   Forms of Religion, forms of Government,
Ideal Arts, Benefit Institutions, Sciences, all the busy
work of the world that is not wholly connected with
objects of sense, is the product of this activity.

The ego as it enters on this state of life begins to
realise that—

> "To dignify the day with deeds of good
> And constellate the eve with noble thoughts,
> This is to live , and let our lives narrate
> In a new version solemn and sublime
> The grand old legend of humanity."

SECTION III.

THE POLAR-OPPOSITE FORMS OF THE THIRD GROUND.
THE OND AND ONDE COROLLAS

THE starting-point of the evolution of the first
ground was the neutral form of the Onden ; this was
differentiated as Ond and Onde by the proportional
scale progression.   The form of the third ground also
is differentiated into the Alpha and Omega antithesis,
male and female, or positive and negative, by means of
proportional progression, as in figures 1 and 2.   The
neutral form of this ground would be what might be

called an Onden Cone, the activity moving upwards in
a straight line, and the form developing from the starting-point of this line and expanding along the line in
a progressively increasing circle; the terms of the
scale of progression which governs the development
being equal, 1, 1, 1, 1, etc.

This circular expansion has taken the place of the
angular expansion of the first ground. The faculties
of sense, the rational attributes of the ego, are no
longer compared among themselves, but are all subordinated to the central idea, and are allowed free exercise as the servants or instruments of the higher
life.

This higher life is progressively realised by means
of appropriate determinations. The first blind impulse to do good soon becomes rationalised in a
greater or less measure, probably according pretty
closely with the scale of rationality the ego had
developed on the lower ground. The antithesis of
the alpha and omega forms becomes apparent. The
alpha or positive form expands from a point into a
trumpet-shaped figure; the omega or negative form
contracts from a circle to a bell-shape, as in figures
1 and 2. There is no generic name for such forms,
though they are strictly mathematical, and are the
basis of innumerable natural forms, especially of the
corollas of flowers, whence it is that Mr. Betts names
them the Ond and Onde Corollas.

The diagrams 1 and 2 are the type forms of this
ground There is in them a double circuit of activity,
the circuit of the internal and that of the external life.
In these examples the two circuits are represented as

equal, the expansion of the corolla equals its height, but they may bear any different proportion one to the other.

In the formulæ by the side of the figures, A and Ω denote as before that the forms are respectively Ond and Onde   F, that they are in a scale of progression having six terms   Λ 1, that it is arithmetical, common difference 1.

Once more there is no undeterminateness manifest in the form   For a time the ego feels as if in the gladness of the performance of duty its ideal was being realised.

Frequently not all the life-energy of the form is conditioned by the determinants of duty. In such a case the remaining activity falls back upon the method of the lower ground, and is determined by the law of pleasure, for since the impulses of the ego are inherent impulses they are regarded as the expression of the Divine will, and are allowed free exercise in subordination to the new law, and not forcibly held in check as on the former standing-ground. The essential life of the form is determined in three dimensions by the law of duty; the superabundant energy is determined in two dimensions by the law of pleasure, and extends itself outwards, forming a kind of foliation, a fringe of personal enjoyment, about the true life— as in forms 3, 4 ; 5, 6 ; 7, 8 : and since other egos are the usual determinants, on this ground this efflorescence may be taken as representing an inclination towards social pleasures and recreation. Figures 3 and 4 are developed according to scales F and H. Scale F determines the work   The difference between F and H conditions two circles of determination as pleasure. "$\phi\cdot75$" indicates that the amount of expansion of this form is to the extension of the axis in the proportion of 3 to 4. This is one example of variation; any other relative proportion may equally well be taken: When the activity of extension predominates it may imply that the inward thought is in excess of the outward action When the reverse is the case, that the life is rather busy than contemplative.

"$\chi\,5$" shows that in this particular form there are five main differentiations of pleasure which are represented as equal. It must be borne in mind that the representations are type-forms, not individual existences The forms of actual life, though they might approximate more or less to the symmetry of the diagrams, would never perfectly realise the type any more than the flowers do The corolla may be five-petaled or three-petaled, or otherwise divided, but these petals will invariably differ, sometimes slightly, sometimes very widely, one from another Figs 5 and 6 have the formula $\frac{\mathrm{D}}{\mathrm{H}}\,\phi2\,\chi\frac{3}{4}$.
$$\mathrm{A}^{\cdot1}$$

Scale D represents the impulse of duty. The difference between D and H is determined as pleasure. $\phi2$ shows that the expansion of the external life has double the energy that the extension of the internal life has. $\chi\frac{3}{4}$ indicates that there are three main divisions of pleasure which are further differentiated in four modes, represented by reflected radii, as in the Ond forms of the first ground. The scale of progression is arithmetical, common difference $\cdot1$, a very low scale of progression. Altogether this pair of diagrams

represent an inferior order of consciousness of this
ground   Figures 7 and 8 are constructed in precisely
the same manner as 5 and 6 ; their formula is $\frac{D}{G} \phi 2 \chi \frac{5}{3}$,
                                                    A1.
consequently they show a slight advance on the former
pair.

The ratio of progression of the ascending activity is,
according to some proportionally diminishing scale,
from the starting-point upwards for the Ond Corollas,
and in the reverse direction for the Onde Corollas.
This is so because the impulses of the ego are no
longer the positive factor in the evolution of the Ond.
They are negative or passive, having subordinated
themselves to the determining law of the higher life,
which now becomes the positive or dominant element
in consciousness   The impulses of the emotional life,
become positive, and the activity which determines
them negative in the Onde.   The progressive circles
of expansion proceed according to an accelerating
ratio as before, outwards for the Ond and inwards for
the Onde.

Just as the impulse of the lower life was progressively realised as the fruition of personal desire in
determined forms of intellect and emotion, so now the
impulse of the higher life begins to be realised in the
alpha and omega forms as the satisfaction of impersonal
desire or Love.   Duty becomes the objective form, and
Conscience, the emotion of duty, the subjective form of
the consciousness.   The external and internal activity
of the ego is determined by the altruistic law of
determination to virtuous thought and action.   In
what measure the activity is thus determined in that

same measure the thought and action react upon the ego as Conscience, the faculty of judgment, sifting, examining, and discerning the motives of conduct and relating the action and thought to the ego in the progressive qualification of consciousness. The impulse of the ego in the Ond Corolla is governed by a scale of diminishing progression, because it is not active but passive, having subordinated itself to the determining law, which it regards as the Divine will. The reactionary impulse of the ego in the Onde Corolla has become active, and by the action of the determinants, the other egos, upon itself they become related to one another, and the ground is prepared for future unity.

Since three-dimensional forms cannot be correctly represented on a flat surface, Mr. Betts has adopted a system of isometrical projection for his diagrams of the third ground in order that the several activities may be measured according to scale. The circles of expansion which appear to lie flat along the axis of ascension should be turned round through a right angle so as to surround the axis. Fig. 16, which is an ordinary elevation, gives a truer idea of the corolla form. He makes use of a series of circles for the expansion in order to simplify the diagrams, but in reality the section of the corolla would be circular, elliptical, or irregular, in accordance with the development of the Ond on the lower grounds. Such irregular expansion would render the delineation of the form very complicated, the work of days instead of the work of a few moments; therefore it is omitted, as the types can be sufficiently well represented without it

SECTION IV.

VARIATIONS OF THE THIRD STANDING-GROUND.
HORN COROLLAS.   BI-AXIAL COROLLAS.

In the first dawn of the new life and the gladness
that accompanies the first exercise of the powers of
soul the ego does not perceive any disproportion
between its ideal and the possibility of realising it.
It contemplates the needs of humanity, which are its
determinants, the non-ego through which its ideal of
duty is realised, but it is not saddened at the sight of
sorrow, and suffering, and ignorance, and want, for they
afford a field for the exercise of its powers ; it believes
that it shall be happy itself and shall make others happy.

If the consciousness is but low in the scale the
determinants are probably the personal needs of those
immediately surrounding it.   Perhaps it is in the
faithful performance of family duties that the ego
feels its ideal shall be realised.   In a consciousness of
a higher order the desire might take the form of
becoming a local benefactor   Thence it might expand
to patriotism and humanitarian schemes for the good
of the nation   In the highest natures the aim would
be universal philanthropy, the raising and benefiting
of mankind generally.

The dotted line of activity ascending from the
central point, the personal ego, may be regarded as
the line of faith and aspiration, the impulse of the
higher life which yields itself up to be determined by
that law which it feels to be divine   As the activity

spreads outwards and becomes determined through other egos a sphere is afforded for the realisation of these impulses But after a time a disproportion begins to manifest itself between the actual possibility of the ego which is absolutely limited at any particular moment of time and the perfectness of its determining law. If the personal limit be considered as 1, the demand upon it would be 1 + if duty is to be performed as perfectly as conceived of.

In the Ond, figure 9, the determining law, the spiritual Will, is felt to be equal to 1·05. That is what the ego conceives that duty requires of it, but its personal power is limited and may be expressed as 1·00. Consequently it never can perfectly do the thing it would. Some compromise has to be effected between the two. The ideal axis, the aspiration, remains unchanged, but the real axis of the consciousness and the form along with it becomes bent or warped from the direct line The best actions are seen to fall short of the standard An incurable sorrow, a sense of sin and failure, accompanies every manifestation of activity. Thus suffering, the great Educator, again takes its place as a factor in the evolution. The disproportion between the ideal and the real again forces itself upon the consciousness. Figure 10 is the emotional counterpart of this form, the real form of this particular conscience, which is not a perfectly ideal conscience.

The two forms are developed in scales K M. The difference between the scales is determined as pleasure. The expansion of the form is ϕ·4, or the external life is to the internal in the proportion

E

of ·4 to 1. The contour, $\chi\frac{5}{2}$, is divided into five main groups of activity, which are further differentiated each into two. Figures 11, 12, are similar forms, but developed from scales M K instead of K M   The difference between the two, instead of spreading outwards as a foliation of pleasure, turns inwards as a determination of pain. The man's spontaneous impulse to action is equal to K, but his action must be determined as M. Consequently he works under compulsion. The necessity that his nature should obey its law compels him to do more work than he desires. In the omega form probably this would appear as an over-scrupulousness and over-sensitiveness of conscience amounting to disease.

Every activity is polar, and has its positive and negative elements, its principles of action and reaction. The activity of Thought and its outward reflection in Work have also their negative element and negative results. When any particular line of Thought and Action is pursued in addition to its positive results it has the negative result that some opposite line of Thought and Action has not been pursued. But besides this the particular line which has been pursued, or rather the particular capacity which has been manifested in a certain way, may be made up of positives and negatives; for the form of an individual life is determined not only by the positive action, which, although falling short of ideal perfection, is yet right action, but also by inaction, by mistaken action, by wrong action. As the evolution of the third ground developes, this opposition becomes increasingly manifest in the consciousness. The axis becomes, as it were, split into two, into positive and negative elements, which do not synchronise These two poles might, peihaps, be called Struggle and Repentance On the proportion of these two elements and the hiatus of undetermined desire between them the internal character of the form depends, and the outward form manifests the internal character in the strange twists and contortions of some of the corolla forms.

In the Onde Corolla, figure 13, the personal limitation is taken as equal to 10. The omega element of the axis is taken as 10 3, and the alpha element as 11·0 Both the positive and negative activity is governed by the scale of F, arithmetical progression, common difference 5. The expansion of the form is taken as ϕ·5, or one-half the extension of the axis. The contour is unbroken χ 1, and the deviation of the real axes from the ideal is δ 2 15—*i e.*, bears that proportion to the whole axis "δ" stands for deflection.

The advanced forms of the third ground are rather complicated It is not easy either to follow the mechanical working or to fully grasp the significance of the Representation. Mr. Betts, in one of his letters, gave the following directions for the construction of the Onde, figure 13 :—

" The tracing having formula $\Omega \begin{smallmatrix} \omega 10\cdot3 \\ a11\cdot0 \end{smallmatrix}$ F $\phi5$ $\chi1$ δ 2 15, is as simple an example of the advanced third dimensional ground as I can give. Draw the major axis of the figure fiom F through Ω and the minor F' Ω; divide Ω F according to scale F of A·5 progression, and set off at right angles through the divisions, lines 1, 2, 3, 4, 5, 6. Then, taking a scale of which Ω F measures 10 parts (scale used is half-inch to a part), and placing its zero at Ω advance the other end along F 6 until 10 3 is reached and draw Ω 10 3, then advance it to 11 0 and draw Ω 6, the intersections Ω 1, 2, &c., and Ω 1', 2', &c., will give proportional lengths of scale F, A·5, enlarged to ω 10·3 and α 11·0. Next mark off F' in terms of ϕ 5, that is half Ω F, and divide according to scale F. Upon Ω X mark off a point "x" equal to 2·15 of scale used—this is δ (deflection) of the formula. I call the dotted systems of centres from F to x a "cyme," that word having approximate (botanical) meaning for its use You ask what rule determines the form of the curve? I reply on this ground it appears quite arbitrary, as appertaining to the next or fourth dimension it as yet is indefinite, and you are at liberty to make use of any curve you may think proper for the cyme To illustrate this by the similar instance of the transition from the first to the third ground, whence came the form of the corolla? We found its origin on the first ground in the whorl of leaves around the stalk; or, speaking morally, the pursuit of pleasure in a continued series of objects. Now this pursuit, or the appearance of leaves successively at the growing point of a stalk, could not possibly be determined by any law of the first ground, but by one beyond it may Upon the first ground it appeared as a change in the object, and so we find leaves always appear at right angles to the last double set or in opposition to a single leaf—the whorl does not arrange around the stalk till afterwards, and does not become a fixed law of form until the bud metamorphosis appears So also the cyme on the third ground is arbitrary, and if you were to fix it by a series of co-ordinates, which would be quite possible, yet these would stand for nothing other than the fact, also manifested in the arbitrary curves, that the two activities of the form are mutually antagonistic as well as in unison, and that indeed all varieties of corolla forms are essentially due to this antagonism, and without it no real life would be possible; we should all be, more or less, *perfect* and useless If, therefore, you have already delineated corollas without this evident conflict, it means simply that the scales are so nearly perfect that you have not represented the antagonism Every step we take brings us nearer to the exact conditions of life, all intermediate forms being more or less ideal, and therefore not *real*. If, therefore, you are copying the diagram in hand you will trace off the curves F ω x, F a x, and you will find by dividing them into (say 12) parts, they will equal the lines Ω 6, Ω 10 3 (but if you are taking a flower from the fields you will draw your cyme as near as you think such a one as will produce the corolla required). On these cyme curves mark off the distances Ω 10 3 on the a curve and Ω 11 0 on the ω curve as nearly as you can by sub-division of the parts to allow for the curve These will be your new centres. About centres on F ω x curve describe the semicircles 1 1, 2·2, 3·3, &c., with radii taken from scale Ω F and about centres on F a x describe semicircles 1 5, 2 4, 3·3, &c., with radii taken from the same scale. The contour of the form, χ, is unbroken, F being a simple scale. Draw in the vertical contour by lines tangential to the circles and the form is complete."

In the following diagrams, figures 14, 15, compound scales are used in the condition of χ, a prominent feature of the form   The method of construction is the same as in the preceding diagrams   The use of semicircles as scaffolding for the form instead of elliptical or trapezoidal curves will not interfere with the process of construction, which shows the activities operating.

The obverse form of this ground is an Onden Cone when a simple scale is used, and a sort of irregular pyramid when compound scales are taken   To avoid complication this has been omitted.   It corresponds to the effect of the work done in life.   If the Onden of the first ground, the causal form, resulted in a mere phantom of sense-production, this result is one of permanent effect, both in ourselves and also in that we leave behind us our mark on the earth

The conflict within him at last compels man to contemplate life on this plane as a whole, and the ever-widening disproportion he perceives between his powers and possibilities again impel him on towards a higher plane.   He perceives that not in philan-thropic work, not in intellectual thought, not in per-sonal virtue, shall his idea become realised.   The blooming corolla of fiery activity fades and perishes, shrivelling away into an unsightly rag, and man is left once more heart-sick and bereft of all, to seek, if so be he may find it, the way of life and truth.

SECTION V.

SPECULATIONS ON A FOURTH DIMENSION IN SPACE.

BEFORE proceeding to the evolution of the fourth ground, it is necessary briefly to consider the subject of a possible fourth-dimension in space.

Mr. Francis Galton made the following remarks on the subject of "attention" in an article published in the "Nineteenth Century Magazine."—"The wheel of a moving carriage is drawn in a blur, with, however, numerous radial streaks, showing, if I mistake not, that attentive observation is never continuous, but acts in rapid pulses, so that the revolving wheel is seen in many momentary positions. I have endeavoured in this way to measure the intervals between the successive throbs of close attention."

This seems to be equivalent to saying that when we look around and see the three-dimensional space appertaining to our material universe this seeing is not continuous but alternate. We positively see, and negatively not see, in successive instants, as our consciousness vibrates into the external world and returns thence again.

Suppose a man were able to reverse the poles of his attention and make what was positive negative and what was negative positive, it is conceivable that he might not-see this material world and look at something else . . . . and, if so, what? Since three dimensions exhaust the limits of extension it can be conceived that he might see space in three dimensions again; but space of an opposite quality to that with which he is habitually familiar.

In the occasional accidental occurrence of second
sight and other interior senses, in some of the phenomena of Spiritualism, in the traces of genuine occultism
which may be found in the literature, especially the
sacred literature, of all nations and times we have
any record of, we have evidence of the possibility of
such an alternative space-perception; of seeing, hearing, etc, in a world not perceptible to the ordinary
senses   In the language of occultism the five subtle
senses with which we perceive the more interior
quality of space are called the astral senses—*i.e.*, clairvoyance, clair-audience, and touch, taste, and smell on
the astral or ætherial plane of matter   Our Saxon forefathers classified the senses as the five wyts and the five
inwyts, but by the inwyts, in all probability, they meant
rather the intellectual faculties than interior senses.

With a consciousness of space in alternating three
dimensional spheres alternately cognised through the
exterior and the interior sense, we might infer as a mathematical certainty the existence of a fourth dimension
in space, although the direct perception of it might
still be impossible to us. We should have actual knowledge of the co-existence of spheres, although we
might still be unable to form a conception of the
nature of the unity in which solids can co-exist as do
planes in the unity of the solid   In four dimensional space solidity must be merged and become non-
existent otherwise than as the mere surface appearance,
so to speak, of a more transcendental state, just as we
now perceive plane superficies to be an illusion in
respect to real existence, since it is only an external
attribute of solidity.

Mr. Galton makes use of the child's toy, the Wheel of Life, to illustrate the vibratory character of attention. This toy consists of a broad wheel revolving on a pivot. A series of pictures are arranged round the wheel with a black bar between each When the wheel is revolved slowly we are conscious of a picture, a bar, another picture, another bar, successively But when the wheel is revolved with sufficient rapidity we lose sight of the black dividing bars altogether They pass during the ebb of our attention, and the pictures appear continuous. They are arranged so that the figures in them seem to be moving in concerted action—as, for instance, boys playing leap-frog, or monkeys jumping through hoops. Now suppose that another series of representations were painted in phosphorescent paint on the black bars, when we made the wheel to revolve in light, we should see the series of representations between the bars and not-see the series on the bars. By putting out the light we should in a certain sense reverse the poles of our attention, for we should now see the phosphorescent series on the bars and not-see the series between the bars. We should know that there were two sets of representations, and we should apprehend them ideally as existing together, but we could only have a real perception of them alternately. Sometimes in the twilight it might happen, if the wheel was revolved rather slowly, that we should get the two sets of pictures a little mixed; and the same sort of thing occurs with clairvoyants who occasionally see objects of the inner world among those of the outer world

An interesting article, by Mr Howard Hinton, entitled "What is the Fourth Dimension?"* appeared in one of the latter numbers of the now defunct "University Magazine." Giving the simple mathematical conception commonly accepted of the generation of the square by the motion of a line, and of the cube by the motion of a square, he works out Professor Zollner's suggestion, and imagines Beings whose consciousness is limited to one or to two dimensions of space, and by the comparison of such states of consciousness with our own three-dimensional state, reasons out from analogy what must be some of the conditions of a state of four-dimensional consciousness But he has not taken into account what may be not inaptly termed "the intermediate state" of consciousness, in which the co-existence of solids would be perceived through the alternation of spheres of perception, but the four-dimensional unity in which they subsist would not yet have become apparent.

Mr Betts's conception of the generation of dimensions differs to some extent from the received mathematical one which Mr. Howard Hinton makes use of According to Mr Betts's system the activity of a point generates the line as a positive activity and negative re-activity which are the ground of polarity. The simple line has no direction, for direction implies relation, and there is nothing yet to be related to But the line having been generated let us suppose a further

---

* This article has since been reprinted as No. 1 of a series of Scientific Romances by Mr. Hinton, published by Swan, Sonnenschein & Co.

activity of the point, which yet is not a repetition of
the former. This must necessarily generate a second
line, and thus the plane comes into existence but only
ideally or potentially, its existence is implied in the
co-existence of lines, but it has not yet become manifest as surface. Just so the existence of a four-
dimensional state is implied in the co-existence of
alternating three-dimensional ones

"Really speaking" (we quote from a letter of
Mr. Betts) "our conception of objects can only be
defined as successive changes in time of the same
mathematical point ; but by the power of Imagination,
which we call Intuition, we are enabled to hold in
one result three consecutive laws and think them in-
stantaneously." (Mr. Betts employs the word law after
a fashion of his own, as here, "three laws," to denote
three opposite modes of activity) "Now, can we conceive of a fourth dimension in Intuition ? I think we
can, theoretically but not practically, in our present
sphere of existence. Suppose yourself the centre of a
sphere of three dimensions, in any direction through
which you can project length, breadth, and depth, could
you not reverse the process, and from the confines of this
sphere contract depth. breadth, and length to a point in
your consciousness? Would not this be a new dimension co-existent with the other three? What would
it amount to? The point to which you retire is not
merely the point from which you started, it has now
the content of the other three dimensions though
contracted to a point—that is, you have now the
capacity of extension into and out of spheres generally, and your central point of consciousness

becomes the portal to the universe of spheres around
you."

The possibility of such a projection of the consciousness into and out of spheres constitutes the
stage of human evolution which Mr. Betts calls the
fourth standing-ground.   But the actual realisation of
a four dimensional state of consciousness belongs to
the fifth ground, which is the positive ground of life,
whereas the fourth is only a negative and intermediate one.

SECTION VI

THE FOURTH STANDING-GROUND OF LIFE

A BEING living on the surface of a solid, and unable
to cognise anything but surface, would imagine that
surface had a real existence, and would ascribe to it
certain qualities which belong to the solid; but as
soon as the consciousness expanded to the conception
of three dimensions it would become apparent that
surface is absolutely non-existent as a reality.   It is
the veriest Maya, delusion.   Similarly, when the consciousness expands to the conception of four dimensions we may discover that our notion of solidity is
nothing but a figment of the imagination, a mode in
which we have imperfectly conceived of some of the
attributes of transcendental space.

The limited and apparently separate personality of
each of us, and this so-seeming solid globe, may be
but the temporary appearances to our consciousness of
a larger reality which shall be actually perceived on

the higher platform of life, whence we may look back
and perceive the unreality of the transitory personal
life, where

> "All the world's a stage,
> And all the men and women merely players"

The fourth standing-ground of life, like the second,
is a negative and reactionary one, the alternation from
an objective to a subjective stage of evolution.   But,
since the abstract subjectivity must remain for ever
unrealised, any state of subjectivity that is realised
must be only a more interior objectivity. As compared
with the realisation of the more objective state the
alternating subjective state is its opposite; but as
compared with abstract objectivity or subjectivity,
which in truth are one, the concrete objective is mixed
with subjectivity, and the concrete subjective with
objectivity.   In the former objectivity preponderates,
in the latter subjectivity.   It is only a difference of
proportion, for the pendulum of consciousness can
never to all eternity swing quite out of either.

On the third standing-ground the consciousness had
dimly felt the presence of another plane of life than
the physical   By the time the fourth ground is attained
the psychical or astral plane becomes a possible object
of direct perception.   The attention can be directed to
or withdrawn from either plane.   The interior senses
are developed as the foundation of the higher evolution as the exterior senses were developed as the
foundation of the lower evolution—and as the lower
sense was subordinated to intellectual perception, so
the psychic sense becomes the tool of the spiritual per-

ception of the fifth ground   But on the fourth ground,
although the psychic sense may, and indeed must, exist,
and consequently the consciousness is intermediate
between a three and a four-dimensional development,
being able to cognise either sensuous or supersensuous
objects, yet the ego feels to have no impulse for the
exercise of either sense.   The hope of realising his
ideal through work has faded, and again he lies at the
" centre of indifference," again he hears " the everlasting nay."

The third ground was a fruitless attempt of the ego
to realise its ideal by work, undertaken with and for
humanity.   The impulses were determined by a power
seemingly external, which was regarded as the Divine
Will.   In the first gush of the ascending activity, when
the life burst forth into flower, it seemed as though
perfect satisfaction was to be gained on this plane, but
as the evolution proceeded, undeterminateness, deep-
seated at the root of life, became increasingly manifest.
An element of failure accompanied even approximate
success.   Imperfection was found to mingle with every
effort of usefulness   An ever-widening chasm yawned
between the apparent possibility and the actual accom-
plishment.   The refuge in action failed.   Reaction
set in again, and the corolla that bloomed so brightly
faded and withered away.

Following the analogy of the growing plant, as the
Onden was the germ, and the Ond the leaf, and the
form of the third ground the flower, so the next stage
may be compared to the pistil and stamens flung up
into the infinite with an infinite yearning.

The personality was progressively developed on the

earlier standing-grounds of life and culminated on the third, but neither in personal pleasure nor in personal virtue was the ego able to realise its ideal. The fourth ground may be considered as the evolution of negative impersonality. The third ground was a state of busy activity, of doing. The fourth is a state of sorrowful passivity, of not-doing, because the desire is no longer to the act, though action continues mechanically, because virtue has become instinctive. It may be summed up in one word—sacrifice. The ego has given itself up, the personal desires are quenched, and the whole desire of the soul is poured forth in a despairing cry for knowledge—life

Desire compels fruition—and when the soul, from the depth of its sorrow and despair, flings itself forth into the infinite in an infinite passion of longing—then, when the battle of life seems lost, all is won. Spiritual perception awakes and the isolated fragment is received back into the bosom of the All. In the self-forgetfulness of that supreme moment, in the unutterable bliss of that reunion, the sacrifice is accomplished, the self-surrender is complete. Man passes through the gate of death into the only true life, which is not egotism, not altruism, but eternal unity. This transition has been variously called Regeneration—the new Birth—the Beatific vision—Union with the Logos—the threshold of Nirvana.

SECTION VII.

THE FIFTH STANDING-GROUND OF LIFE.

In the reaction of the second ground the point or focus had the content of the plane—*i e.*, the activities of the sense-life. In the reaction of the fourth ground the point or focus has the content of the sphere, the entire physical, intellectual, and moral nature, for reason and virtue have become instinctive, as natural to man as his breathing or the beating of his heart.

As in the transition to the third standing-ground of life the sense-perception of the physical ego became the servant, the instrument, of the psychic ego, so now in the evolution of the fifth standing-ground the metaphysical and ethical perception of the psychic ego, which have now developed their appropriate organs, become the servants and instruments of the higher ego—the machinery, so to speak, of the spiritual ego, the true being, the *I am*, which, as it begins to be recognised as the true self, makes man more than man, for it is a ray of the great I AM, the unposited point, which is everywhere and in All. The evolution of the first ground is Having or Egotism, of the third Doing or Altruism. The evolution of the fifth ground, the culmination of Humanity, is Being or Unity. The three grades of consciousness might be called sense-consciousness, soul-consciousness, and spirit or god-consciousness

But though point after point of knowledge has been won, though realm after realm of ignorance has

been enlightened and numberless barriers of indolence
have been overthrown; though the individual ego
has perceived its oneness with the All, first by faith
through revelation on the earlier grounds of life,
next by reason through inference, as its intellectual
faculties expanded on the third ground, and at last
by actual perception through the purified and exalted
faculties of the higher self as the fifth ground was
reached, yet ever beyond the actual point—however
elevated the position it has attained, and however
extended the circumference embraced by consciousness—lies the unposited point, the Great Unscrutable.
The finite cannot compass the infinite. The lesser
alpha, the individual being, though its identity of
substance with the great Alpha, the All-being, be
disclosed, yet still exists within the circumscribing
circle of Prakriti. Consciously one with the All in
substance, it yet remains consciously separate from
the All in form. But since the limit of Prakriti, the
infinite Omega, is not an actual but an ideal limit,
within which the actual limits of each form may be
for ever and ever extended, there lies before the ego
the possibility of eternal progress, through ever-
heightening cycles of objective manifestation, alternating by reason of polarity with ever intenser states
of subjectivity. And herein lies the joy and glory of
existence, for were it not so, were there fixed a hard
and fast limit beyond which none could pass, that
would be annihilation. Life would culminate in
Death, Hope be quenched in Despair, and Existence,
instead of an everlasting progress towards light,
would become the blank darkness of Desolation

F

While we remain enchained by our personalities on the lower planes of life, scarcely can the imagination prefigure, in faintest outline even, the mysteries of so transcendent a plane of life.   As the first ground was compared to the leaf and the third to the flower, so this may be called the season of fruit, and the fruit has the seed of life in itself, and is therefore immortal

On the fourth ground man becomes negatively impersonal, on the fifth he becomes positively impersonal, for he recognises his personality as not himself, but one particular expression of the forces of Nature He does not act—that is, his personality does not act for its own sake, for he has passed the stage of personal doing impelled by personal desire.   He does not act, but Nature acts in and through him, for he has become a conscious part of Nature, and can rede her runes, and knows her laws.   He has power over matter, for all things are himself, diverse manifestations of the One   He has influence over men, for all men are himself, diverse fragments of the great I AM.   He draws all men up with him, for though he has crossed the threshold of the New Life himself, not until all men have entered into it with him can the unity be fully consummated by the union of humanity in a common subjective life—a life in which, though the centre of consciousness of each remains unchanged, the circumference embraces the consciousness of all mankind, the four-dimensional unity of the individual spheres of consciousness

When the evolution of humanity is thus fully accomplished, mankind will pass away from the material plane of existence into a subjective state of bliss, which is the fruition of man's highest desire. But even this is not final: in the fulness of time humanity, still united in one, as the living cells in one living body, shall emerge thence to pass through new cycles of evolution, culminating, it may be, in the union of our own humanity of this planetary chain with other humanities of other solar systems, and these again combining into yet grander and grander unities in an endless progression through infinite series of development, new and ever larger antitheses of existence being perceived as the former ones are merged in the unity, every taking of the not-I into the I opening the way to grander antitheses—for antithesis is the one imperishable thing without which Being cannot be manifested.

But such speculations are vain; the dim short-sighted eye of man is blinded when it seeks to penetrate the endless vistas of the Beyond.

No representation is possible of the form of consciousness on the fifth standing-ground of life, although being a positive plane it would be representable if we were able to conceive of it. We are able, either according to the laws of Perspective or by some conventional system of Projection, to make a representation of solid form on a surface, therefore if we understood the appearance of matter in a four-dimensional state we might represent it either by means of a system of solid perspective, or by projecting its boundary solids. Mr. Betts arrives by a sort of guess at the condition of four-dimensional matter in this way. He takes a pair of his antithetical forms of the third ground and draws them in opposite directions, so placed that their obverse forms overlap, and by combining these obverse forms by lines through their salient points he gets various shapes of crystals, differing according to the scales of the corollas he uses Hence he infers that matter on the higher plane will be crystalline ; and when solidity is merged in a more transcendent objectivity probably matter will be no longer resistant.

Mr. Betts has also made some interesting experiments in colour by revolving his Onds and Ondes, either the plane or the solid ones, in a beam of strong light let into a darkened room He cuts out the forms in cardboard or zinc. The most pronounced Alpha form possible produces waves of a beautiful crimson colour. The corresponding Omega form a deep blue ; slightly modified forms waves of orange and violet ; while any form in which undeterminateness predominates produces chiefly waves of green, which he regards as the colour of infancy and incompleteness. He conceives that an entrancing colour-music, might be derived from a suitable arrangement of revolving forms. Through such harmonies of colour it might, perhaps, be possible to derive some suggestions for a theory of Sociology. Some of the diagrams have been printed in approximately correct colours.

Mr Betts expects that his theoretical Science of Representation will be complemented by a practical Science of Determination, for he believes that every natural form is a symbol, and if we understood the mystic inscriptions of Nature we might read in every natural form some word of Life.

A Science of Determination would be the foundation of a true system of sociology, in which each form of human kind would take its natural rank in a great spiritual hierarchy He thinks it possible that the key to such a science might be found in the neglected Science of Astrology, to which he has devoted a considerable amount of study; he has himself drawn Horoscopes not unfrequently with success He considers his Science of Representation to be the Alpha Science and that the complementary Science of Determination will be an Omega Science, wherefore he seems to expect that it will be chiefly the task of women to develope it. Perhaps the key will rather be found through the unfolding of the psychic powers of man, whereby the magnetic aura of each individual is perceived clairvoyantly in varying shades of colour in accordance with his quality, for so we might learn to combine harmonies of men The psychic sense being more interior might be called the Omega sense, and the physical sense being more exterior, Alpha.

Forces of any kind, not only the activities of human consciousness, may similarly be represented by diagram.

Mr. Betts has made some studies of the evolution of consciousness in the lower animals. These forms resemble mono-cotyledonous leaves of various degrees of complexity, as the diagrams of human sense-consciousness resemble di-cotyledonous ones. Also he has made some studies of the Solar System, and endeavoured to find the law by which the intervals between the planets are regulated. He considers that the planets mark points of undeterminateness in the

circuit of the polar forces of attraction and repulsion.
Gravitation he considers as the resultant of a proportional relation of these forces and not as an independent force in itself.

He believes the form of the Solar System, by which he means the invisible form of the activities immediately concerned in its production, and of which certain points are marked by the position of the planets, to be a nine-petaled lily similar to the Ond Corollas. Every Solar System in the sky he supposes to be the counterpart of some flower at our feet. Our Solar System is an Alpha or male universe. Others he believes may be Omega or female forms. The systems with dual suns he thinks may resemble his diagrams of bi-axial corollas.

In addition to the consecutive series of diagrams already explained, a few others are given which may be interesting. They have been selected out of an immense number of drawings.

Figure 16 is an ordinary elevation of an Ond Corolla in orthographic instead of isometrical projection. It shows very clearly the coil of undeterminateness, which is coloured red, winding through the form, and the spiral lines of experience or memory encircling the form of the consciousness These lines could not well be drawn in the Corolla diagrams of the other kind of projection.

Figure 17 is the earth and its antithetical form or necessary counterpart, which taken together strangely enough are the same as the ancient astronomical sign for the earth, ♁.

Figure 18 is the nine-petaled lily representing our

solar universe, and figure 19 a plan of the same.
A semi-gaseous or cometary state he considers might
be represented by Ond forms of the first ground

A brief abstract like the present one can give but
a meagre conception of Mr. Betts's Theories and
Diagrams. It will have served its purpose if it shows
that the studies which Mr. Betts has made towards
developing a Science of Representation make clear the
possibility of using mathematics as the handmaid of
metaphysical as well as physical science. In this union
there lies the possibility of a considerable development of thought in the future along various lines
There are many gaps, confusions, and imperfections
in Mr. Betts's work, as no one is better aware than
himself, but he puts it forth as the first step in a new
direction, or at least the first step taken in that direction in our own day, and he hopes that others, abler
than himself, may follow in the same path, and geo-
metrise the laws of the universe more successfully
than he has done.

$\underset{A_1}{A_F}$

Fig. 1.

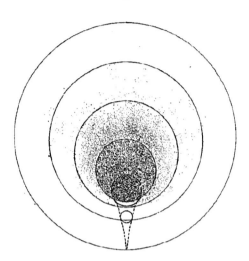

$\underset{A_1}{\Omega_F}$

Fig. 2.

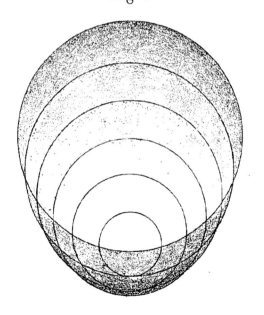

$\mathbf{A}$FH ϕ ⁊5 χ 5
$\mathrm{A_1}$

Fig. 3.

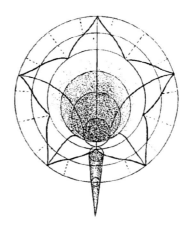

ΩFH ϕ ·75 χ 5
$\mathrm{A_1}$

Fig. 4.

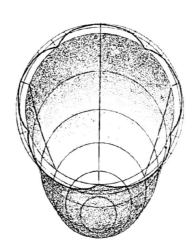

Fig. 5.

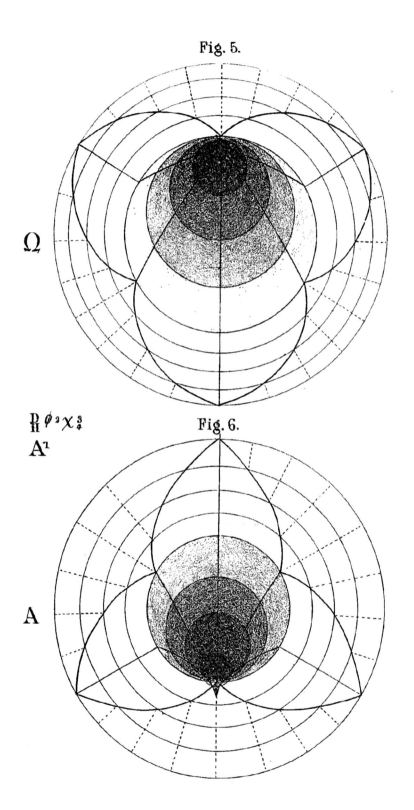

Ω

$\overset{D}{\text{H}} \, \phi^{2} \, \chi^{\frac{3}{4}}$

A¹

Fig. 6.

A

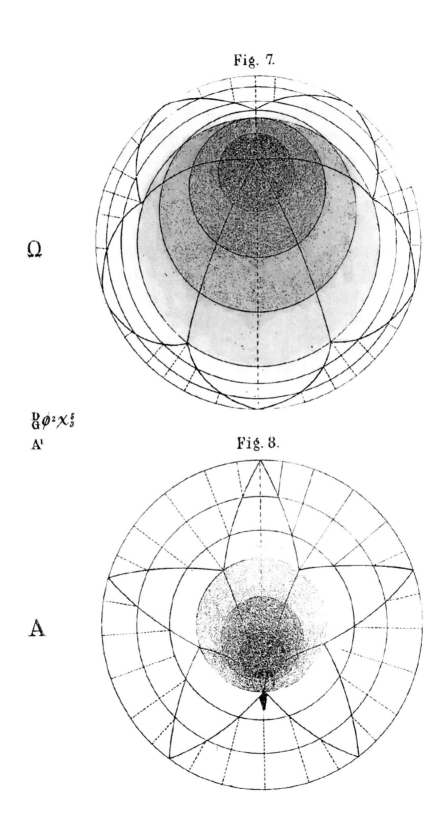

Fig. 7.

Ω

$\begin{smallmatrix}D\\G\end{smallmatrix}\phi^2\chi^5_3$

A^1

Fig. 8.

A

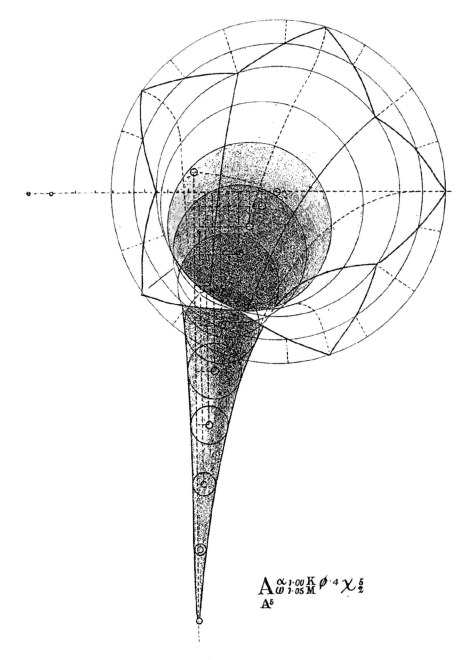

$A^{\alpha\ 1\cdot00\ K}_{\omega\ 1\cdot05\ M}\ \phi\ \cdot 4\ \chi\ \frac{5}{2}$

A^5

Fig. 9.

$\Omega \, {}^{\alpha \, 1 \cdot 00}_{\omega \, 1 \cdot 05} {}^{K}_{M} \phi \cdot 4 \, \chi \, {}^{5}_{2}$
$A \cdot {}^{5}$

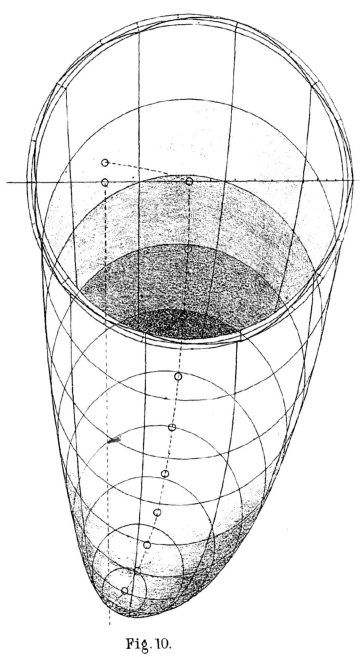

Fig. 10.

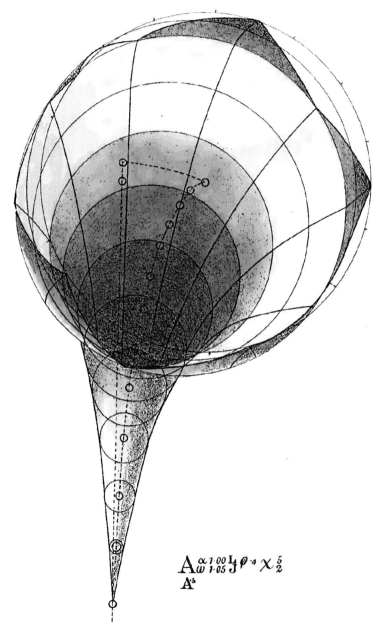

$$A_{\omega\ 1\cdot05}^{\alpha\ 1\cdot00}\ \underset{A^s}{\text{L}}\ \varrho\cdot4\ \chi\ \tfrac{5}{2}$$

Fig. 11.

$\Omega \begin{smallmatrix} \alpha & 1\cdot00 & M \\ \omega & 1\cdot05 & K \end{smallmatrix} \phi \cdot 4 \, \chi \tfrac{5}{2}$
$A \cdot 5$

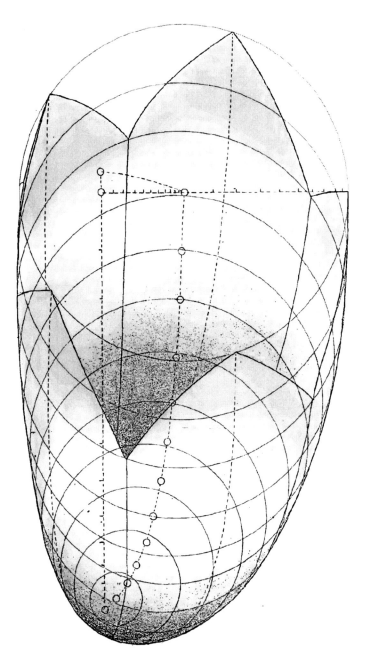

Fig.12.

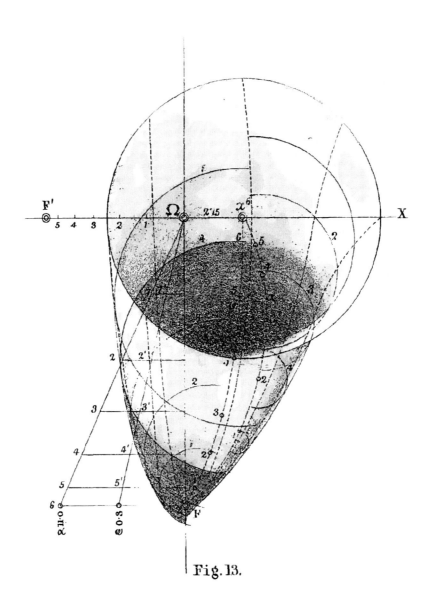

Ω ℧ 10·3 F φ·5 𝒳'δ 2·15
α 11·0
A·5

F'

Ω   2·15   𝒳   X

Fig. 13.

A^{α 10 5} D^{∅ 5} X⁵ δ²
(t) 11 0 H D

A⁵

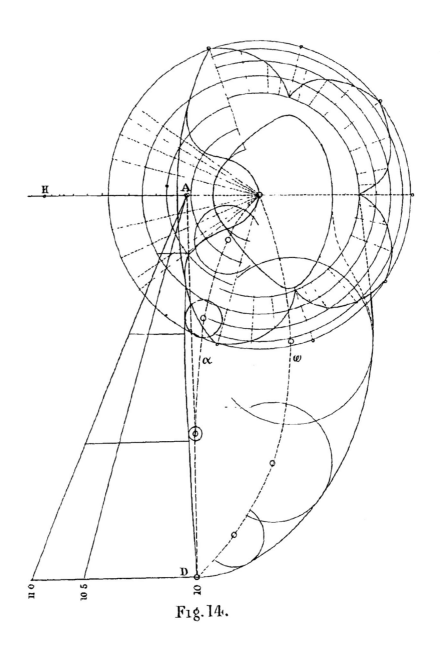

Fig. 14.

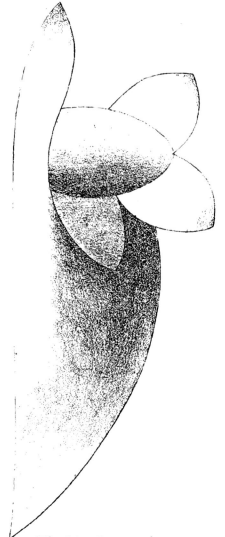

Fig.14. *Perspective appearance.*

(To follow the other Fig 14.)

$\Omega \begin{matrix} \omega \ 10\cdot3 \ H \ \phi \ 3 \ \chi \ 4 \ \phi \ 2\cdot15 \\ \alpha \ 11\cdot0 \ F \ B \end{matrix}$
A·5

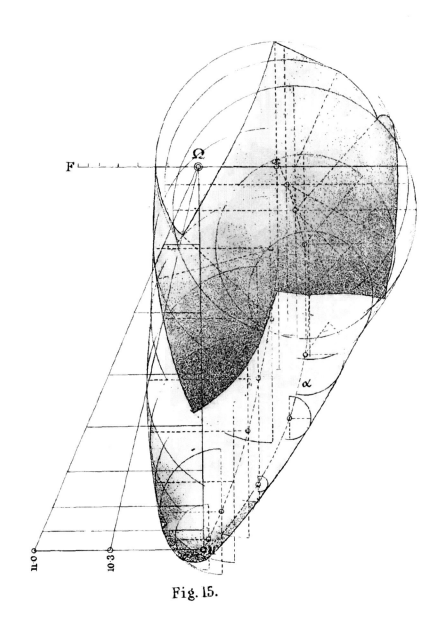

F

Ω

α

11·0

10·3

Fig. 15.

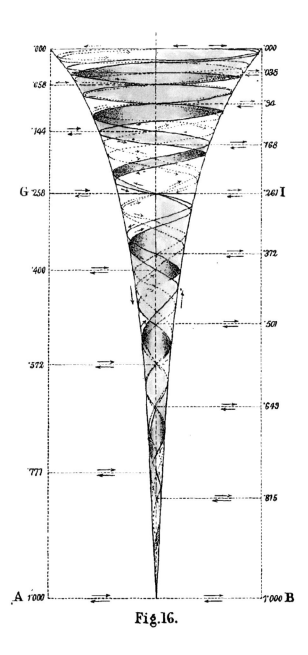

Fig.16.

C.F.Kell.-Lith & Printer, 8, Furnival S⁺ Holborn, London, E.C.

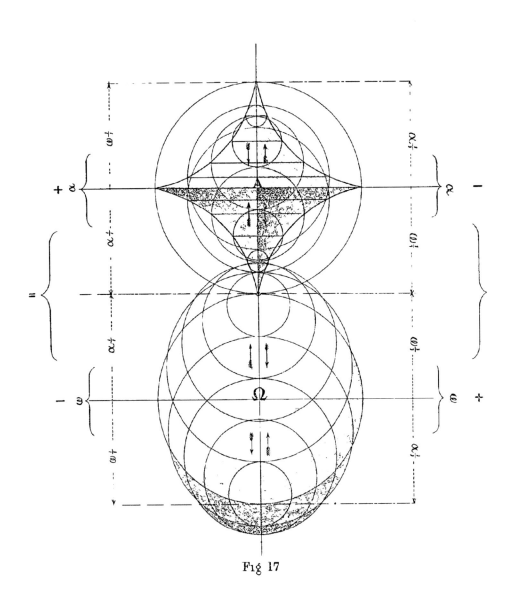

Fig 17

Fig. 18.

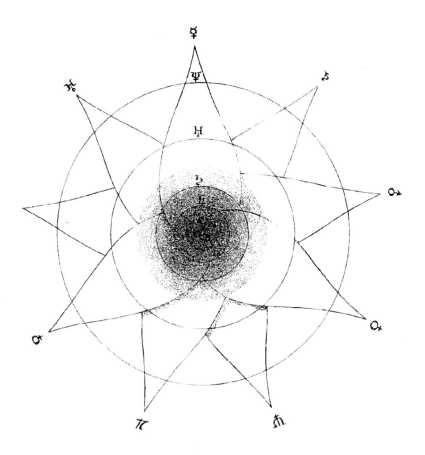

Fig. 19.

APPENDIX

———◇———

Mrs Boole made some allusions to Mr Betts' unpublished diagrams in her book, "Symbolic Methods of Study," and quoted passages from some of his letters Some further quotations from letters are appended here which may be found to be interesting and to throw light on his System of Representation.

Do not imagine that a science of representation has anything to do with other than spirit. If you could see the daily action of your own spirit you would find that it could be as exactly defined and delineated as one of the diagrams. Your body, which is merely the instrument of your spirit (its hands), returns to dust as soon as this spirit ceases to act, why should such a secondary object and servant hide the Eternal from yourself and others. To transparent thought the body disappears as a mist before the sun, and when you are thoroughly able to understand these diagrams and the truths they inculcate, when you look at any forms of humanity it will not be at their outward appearance, neither at their hapless struggles after vanities, but at their unhappy Ideal, which is giving them such trouble, and which they would almost fain be rid of that they might eat and sleep undisturbed.

    *   *   *   *   *

It seems clear to me that Darwin's evolution is really involution, for he terms that the former, which results in a perfect, or nearly so, type. To obtain a type it is necessary for evolution to have ceased and for involution to have set in and crystallised into a species The missing link in his scheme is essentially the mean negative zero from which has eventually sprung the human race—which, because it is negative, could not appear in the world until a condition of nature had arrived when it could be inverted into a positive reproductive activity of Thought From this it would appear that the animal in us is not our true nature, but a stock on which we have been grafted (not before possible) so that humanity may advance to its destiny to reproduce the universe.

      *   *   *   *   *

The generation of the life-cell by means of Thought immediately provokes the question, Does physiology bear it out? To answer this in detail would require an essay on many subjects. Yet we may throw some light on the subject by a bold hypothesis with which many things agree. The analysis of cells in cellulose indicates a combination in definite proportions, always constant, I presume, of hydrogen, oxygen, and carbon, and nitrogen performs a function in the growth of cell-tissue. The three activities which have accompanied us all through the building-up of our forms answer in a remarkable manner to the three former "elements." If we take the active or positing ideal activity as hydrogen we have the determining or passive real activity as carbon, and the synthetical activity of the Imagination in supporting and combining these opposites as oxygen, which, as you are aware, is a supporter of combustion. Further, the negative reactionary activity, which is not contemplated as activity but felt as resistance and gives definite substance to our Thoughts, may be compared to nitrogen, which carries off, as oxygen carries on, the opposite activities of Life. That which, therefore, enters consciousness as "I" is the equilibrium of these opposite activities or elements which cannot be explained but only felt, and we must not confuse the condition of these elements in their pure or uncombined state, with their condition when in action and reaction with one another.

It is undoubted, for instance, that hydrogen and oxygen, in composing water lose all their original characteristics, and that the union is attended with activities too minute for the microscope to detect, and which can perhaps be analysed by correspondence in the human race. If these activities exist the so-called elements interact again in a new and infinite sphere of individualities, and, at the moment of our reducing form to elementary composition, at the same moment our Panorama widens into infinitude, divisible only by Thought, and our hydrogen, carbon, oxygen, and nitrogen dissolve in a flood of Light, tinting it with rainbow colours.

*   *   *   *   *

A true science of Form or Life would proceed from an analysis of the laws of Light as revealed in colour, and then each reflection or personality would become readable and empirically determinable to a general unity, and what we term physical Light would be a true symbol of the internal Light of Thought or Reason. I imagine the difficulty you find in understanding the metaphysical sense of the forms to arise from the strange revelation that our thinking capacity (which you are aware is the only real thing about us) takes the forms of leaves and flowers. If you consider that our present personality is only a form of time and not of eternity, also that the subjective thinking Universe evidently takes these forms, then perhaps you may be able to discern in the distant future of each of us an objective sphere of such thinking forms in which our personality in regard to its form will merge in an Infinite Form, while in regard to its essence (as we see in our own solar universe) such a condition would be one in which Reflection itself (which we are) would no longer present an impenetrable barrier between us and the Infinite, but would be thoroughly transparent to itself and rendered sensitive to the tones of an Infinite harmony.

*   *   *   *   *

It is not true that there is an Earth in space with individuals wandering about on it; it is not true mathematically, but each

carries its own world with it, and if there is any ground of
relation between my world and your world or other worlds, that
ground exists in you or me and not in the world, except only
as it is a part of each independently.

* * * * *

This much we can see, that an activity or personality must
be united or merged in its complementary passivity or impersonality if life is again to be life and existent as a unity in a
society of similar unities beyond this earthly sphere.

* * * * *

Have I sufficiently explained the metaphysical meaning of
these diagrams? There is nothing to be portrayed beyond
the third or corolla ground, for here is the limit of Earthly
history. The introduction of the third law into that ground
is the determination of the activity by the conscience presence
of the Divine Will in the Ond form, and by giving this to be
determined in the Onde form. In each case the conscious
presence of the Divine Will is regarded in its first aspect.
The fourth ground, which is the actual reception and inter-
change of this Divine activity, is unrepresentable like the
second ground, and if we go on to the objective accomplish-
ment of the fourth ground (objective to the individual but
invisible to terrestrial vision), we finally arrive at the fifth, or
ground of science, or perfect knowledge, which I have stated
to be accomplished in the reduction of all human form to a
number and a harmony as the element of the sphere music of
a Universe.

* * * * *

This is not a poetical term, it is Science when I repeat that
Love is the *Substance* of all things, the reactionary activity of
the Intelligence, the solid substratum of the Objective Universe; this, too, is not a figure of speech, but an all-embracing
reality, which gives to existence its eternal standing-ground
and unites all together, so that we think we see the same
world, hear the same sounds, walk the same path, clasp the
same hands, when reason tells us it cannot be so, but each
invents or produces that which it thinks, and the centre of all

our communication is the hidden pavilion of Absolute Being
This is clearing the ground for the apprehension of the fact
that the movements of celestial bodies are the thinking products
of a personal intelligence in advance of terrestrial form.

* * * * *

I have often stated that I was not looking for leaves or
flowers when I commenced my studies, and the coincidence of
their forms with the laws of representation struck me as very
remarkable, and then it at length became clear that these
forms have all along been showing to us the secret which all
have been trying to arrive at—viz., the laws of Being manifested in existence.

* * * * *

For Wisdom and Love are the two counterparts towards
which all are tending, and their apotheosis is not of to-day
but for ever.

* * * * *

Consider your own consciousness of life, day after day, year
after year, with all its apparent changes, joys and sorrows,
and your own consciousness of personality clinging as to the
centre of these unending changes—what would be a Geometrical representation of such an outward life or activity?
As a continuous, never-ending line doubtless, but the unchanging personality remaining through the whole (which
nevertheless you could not define other than as a mere
feeling), this line would appear to gyrate round a centre, your
personality. Further, as this personality appears not to be
stationary entirely, but to be progressing or retrogressing, this
carrying its daily and yearly experiences with it resolves
actual consciousness into a spiral route, which I have shown
is the line of projection of the corolla.

Was it not long ago prophesied that the Lord our God
would come and dwell among us? Lo! He is here amongst
us as He has always been. His thoughts revealed in every
leaf, every flower that blooms; a visible language, the first
and last letters alone of which I have deciphered, and which

Science may fill in by Conquest. We no longer want God-inspired men to reveal His Will, it is all laid out here for us at our feet. We want men and women with eyes (not telescopes or microscopes) to teach us henceforth the Will of the Eternal and the laws of harmonious society. If you were a bright star in the firmament would you be happy there without knowing all about your adjoining brightnesses and systems? Well, each flower tells you a new solar system, and each new flower is a reflection of a developed intelligence arrived in Heaven.

*   *   *   *   *

A grain of sand has life or it would not obey the law of gravitation.

*   *   *   *   *

The negation of a colour is not colourlessness but complementary colour.

*   *   *   *   *

A straight line can alone be truly defined as an infinite determination of activity.

*   *   *   *   *

This frail attempt to solve the problem of life may seem unmeaning, but when we come to understand that all life is an undulatory activity, and that colour is an infinite array of varying undulations, it may perhaps expand into real insight by our tracing the various and infinite permutations of this principle through all states and conditions of existence in the Garden of Eden, whose flowers are human beings, and thus we get back to that Garden from which our ancestor was so abruptly expelled.

*   *   *   *   *

Only after close study and almost endless experiment does light suddenly burst in upon the subject. When such occurs I have always felt and inwardly acknowledged that the flash has come from a higher world. But without the study and experiments I feel sure (I have proved it also) that no light would come. The idea was and is " I and Thou." How to explain this and thereby to explain everything was my problem, for I placed this as the central idea of Existence, the second act of the "I am that I am." And I have found that the diagram floral forms have been, as it were, the Cotyledons on which this idea has subsisted during its unfolding.

It seems to me the great want in the present day is a practical view of life, for you cannot call that life which does not live, and if all could see a symbol of their life in every flower that grows (a true symbol, as I have been trying to show) they would probably soon see more beauty in life than they had done. And if to this the *sudden* knowledge should come of the hidden unity of all, what a ground would they find for living outgoing activity.

* * * * *

Human intelligence is demonstrable by Geometric forms as Symbols of Thought in a definite and, to a certain extent, an absolute manner, in a series of evolutions, commencing at the first stages in the mental faculties of a child, and developing to the completed thinking apparatus of the adult, as it culminates in the Corolla form. By reference to astronomical motions we observe also that these mathematical laws of thought are there clearly embodied in actual living systems, proving that the form of human intelligence is a microcosm of the solar system, showing thereby that this solar system is also the form of a higher-thinking intelligence of which we are but reflections, and clearly embodying a personality. But this personality, whether human or solar, is but a stage of development towards a higher unity, in which personality disappears except as a colour harmony; the whole, Light, being living activity unpersonified except as colour. This higher stage of development follows on the union of the Absolute Alpha and Omega principles, each of which had hitherto been personified as individualisation, and thereby cast out of the internal harmony—the return to this unity with a taint or tint of personality being the higher ideal to which humanity may aspire.

* * * * *

Therefore, also, Wisdom is Thought, and Love is Thought, and if we are to judge between them as to the opposite characteristics of Alpha and Omega we are driven back to our evolution to show how each is necessary and the groundwork of the other.

    *   *   *   *   *

All around we see the flower families, reflections of the starry universe, dumb hitherto except to botanical worms ; how soon shall we commence to cultivate our flower human families, and generalise and specialise them—perhaps discover links between a family here and a constellation there ; a sungod there and a sun-family here ?

    *   *   *   *   *

It may be that here and there a distinguished pure soul (already belonging to a higher sphere) obtains entrance into the highest, but what about the multitude that has to plod the road thither—concerning whom not one is to be lost ? We have invented steam-engines to transport the body with speed, and telegraphs to wing our words, but what spiritual engines have yet been thought out to speed the soul onwards ?

    *   *   *   *   *

The action of the primary and essential spirit body on the natural body, controlling it and rendering it more or less a true symbol of itself, is represented in the natural leaves and flowers around us. Take any leaf, say an elm leaf; you will observe that while all elm leaves partake of a certain form so near as to identify them as elm leaves yet the particular being or growth of each leaf is considerably different. I call the ideal elm leaf that which stamps the leaf as an elm leaf the spiritual body of the leaf, and the actual leaf growing up to this form through endless varieties of being the natural body of the leaf.

    *   *   *   *   *

The true judgment of a vortex, which life is, could only be thoroughly understood by seeing the varying powers in conflict, causing it to swerve now in this direction, now in that, which

I think is just the sort of experience which all find life to be, the final net result being only seen when the conflict is passed and a new sphere is attained. The main result of this teaching would be the lesson inculcated by our forefathers, that of courage, for to the coward they assure us there is nothing in store but Night and the Pool.

* * * * *

Our solar system is the objective plane of the Higher power of whom we are symbols—Earth or Planetary condition being the Onden matter of the Central Spirit, which (*i.e.*, matter) we have shown to be, not dead, inert, but living reaction of Thought. On this subject I may call your attention to the possible and very frequent dislocation of an advanced third dimensional corolla through gross undeterminateness of scales and its possible correspondence with the interplanetary state between Mars and Jupiter in our own Solar system. The corollas of our orchids show very vast dislocations. It may also explain the numerous deaths in infancy, the cyme undeterminateness being the weak or disease point of human constitutions, showing, also, that the death of the form in infancy may be a sign of a still higher birth than that of those reckoned more fortunate who survive. It may yet be possible to determine within what limits of undeterminateness human forms can survive, and discover a law underlying even the survival of the fittest.

* * * * *

"Esoteric Buddhism" appears to me to be the very book needed to complement my studies. . . . But I must now commence with an extract from "Esoteric Buddhism" to show how it so exactly counterparts the Science of Representation. On page 176 are these words:—"The one imperishable thing in the universe which universal pralayas themselves pass over without destroying is that which may be regarded indifferently as space, duration, matter, or motion, not as something having these four attributes, but as something which *is* these four things at once." Now what is this which is these four things at once but our *Onden* differentiated as

G

Ond and Onde? Further than this, we actually discover which are the purely masculine and feminine activities in this Eternal Universe; the Alpha activity, in its infinite representation, is the straight line = duration or Time; the Omega is Space, or Time determinable in this or that method or mode of representation. Matter the simple opposition of the Thinking activity, or that which is Thought, is the reaction of representation, and as matter is described with these or those attributes in Space, it may be termed the Omega reaction *par excellence*, while motion is the Alpha principle *par excellence*, being the progression in time of continued material evolutions. These laws of intuition are not inherent in something, but are that thing itself, and thus the basis of our life is eternal and imperishable as the universe. . . . But can you carry the idea of the A Ω across that gap in the fifth round of humanity (about mid career) where only the really spiritual thought can climb? It is visible in every corolla you examine, it is the transition of petals into stamens and pistil, through which metamorphosis alone the A and Ω spirit thought can enter Nirvana. Here stood Schopenhauer's ideal, cast forth into the infinite blackness, and, as I understand, he never found out that his Alpha had an Omega ideal in the same root.

*   *   *   *   *

The laws of mathematics are absolute and final within themselves, they are *certain* so far as any knowledge can be certain, but the fundamental law of the Science of Representation is that of the *undeterminateness* of Form; hence absolutely *uncertain;* and human formulæ are (as I have before stated) best represented by algebraic surds, there always being an irresolvable remnant, and hence they are called *irrational* quantities. But mathematics placed on a metaphysical basis might be productive of something, certainly they will not till then.

I am firmly of opinion that all sickness and constitutional weaknesses are very quickening of spiritual impulses both to the patient and the others concerned, all the essentially *human*, as opposed to the animal qualities, are mainly strengthened or may be so, and I think sickness might almost take the place in human evolution that natural selection does in the animal world.

*   *   *   *   *

There appears to me to be a fundamental antithesis between Eastern and Western Thought. This would only be carrying out the necessary conditions of all existence, without which Existence would lapse in Being. . . . . Western Thought has sprung from the Hebrew " I am," crude and arbitrary at its first promulgation, but subdued, and humanised, and spiritualised in its latest announcement, so that now this Western idea is taking root as a demand for harmony, and is breaking out on all sides as emotional activity, and is even getting quite unanswerable in its demand, but let but the Lily show herself and you will find a wonderful change come over modern history. A sudden breeze springing up, our ship shall again obey her helm and spring forward toward her horizon.

THE END.

LONDON
PRINTED BY JAS WADE, TAVISTOCK STREET
COVENT GARDEN

A Selection

FROM

Mr. Redway's Publications.

GEORGE REDWAY,

15, YORK STREET, COVENT GARDEN, LONDON.

1887.

15, York Street, Covent Garden,

London, *January*, 1887.

12mo, cloth, 2s.

Nature and Law.

An Answer to

Professor Drummond's "Natural Law in the Spiritual World."

GEORGE REDWAY, YORK STREET, COVENT GARDEN.

A NEW NOVELIST.

Fifine:

A NOVEL.

BY

ALFRED T. STORY.

2 Vols., 21s.

GEORGE REDWAY, YORK STREET, COVENT GARDEN.

THE LIFE, TIMES, AND WRITINGS

OF

Thomas Cranmer, D.D.,

The First Reforming Archbishop of Canterbury.

BY

CHARLES HASTINGS COLLETTE.

GEORGE REDWAY, YORK STREET, COVENT GARDEN.

The Life of Philippus Theophrastus, Bombast of Hohenheim,

KNOWN BY THE NAME OF

Paracelsus,

And the substance of his teachings concerning Cosmology, Anthropology, Pneumatology, Magic and Sorcery, Medicine, Alchemy and Astrology, Theosophy and Philosophy.

Extracted and translated from his rare and extensive works and from some unpublished Manuscripts,

BY

FRANZ HARTMANN, M.D.,

AUTHOR OF "MAGIC," ETC.

———

"Paracelsus was a high priest among mystics and alchemists, he left behind him one hundred and six treatises upon medical and occult subjects, which are likely to be read by the curious as long as mysticism remains a necessary study for whoever would trace the developments of civilisation.

"From some considerable acquaintance with the writings of Paracelsus, we can say that Dr Hartmann has made his excerpts from them with a good deal of skill. Students, indeed, should be grateful for this book, despite its setting of Theosophical nonsense, since to read one of Bombast's Latin or German treatises is a very stiff exercise indeed, unless you are well versed in his very recondite terminology.

"Dr. Hartmann has compiled a very full and accurate glossary of occult terms, which will be of great use to future readers of Paracelsus, and for so much he is to be thanked

"Dr Hartmann quotes some of his recipes for transmuting metals and producing the 'electrum magicum' But Paracelsus is the most transcendental of European mystics, and it is not always easy to know when he is writing allegorically and when practically Dr Hartmann says he has tried these prescriptions and found them all right, but he warns the uninitiated against running the risk of blowing themselves up in the endeavour to follow the master's instructions.

"Paracelsus held firmly to the belief of some of the hermetic writers of the Middle Ages, that it is perfectly possible to create human beings by alchemical means; and he even gives directions (in his treatise 'De Natura Rerum') for the production of homunculi

"On the whole, however, Dr. Hartmann has produced a very amusing book, and a book which will have some permanent value to the student of the occult."—*St James's Gazette.*

———

GEORGE REDWAY, YORK STREET, COVENT GARDEN.

Monthly, One Shilling.

Walford's Antiquarian Magazine

AND

Bibliographical Review.

EDITED BY

EDWARD WALFORD, M.A.

*** *Volumes I. to X, Now Ready, price 8s. 6d. each.*

"The excellent archæological monthly"—*Cassell's Art and Literature.*

"This magazine is dear to the hearts of the lovers of antiquities The meetings of the various learned societies are also described . . and a number of articles of both antiquarian and bibliographical interest."—*Nonconformist.*

"There is not much in *Walford's Antiquarian* that any connoisseur in literary curiosities would care to pass over."—*St James's Gazette*

"A work which, under the skilled and scholarly editorship of Mr. Edward Walford, maintains in the best manner its unique character as a medium for lovers of ancient lore."—*Publisher's Circular*

"Full of interesting notes of quaint and curious lore."—*Glasgow Herald* December 15th, 1886.

CONTENTS OF No. 61.

DOMESDAY BOOK.

FROSTIANA

SOME KENTISH PROVERBS.

The LITERATURE of ALMANACKS

"MADCAP HARRY" and SIR JOHN POPHAM.

TOM CORYATE and his "CRUDITES."

NOTES on JOHN WILKES and BOSWELL'S LIFE of JOHNSON.

COLLECTANEA.—Early Italian Prints—Tercentenary of the Potato—Chaucer Discovery—Sir John Soane's Museum—Copyright in Government Publications—Pausanias—The Loan of Manuscripts—Paper Making in 1588—Portraits of Charles Dickens—Hopton Castle—A very Ancient Watch—The Value of Antiquarian Study.

MEETINGS OF LEARNED SOCIETIES.—Society of Antiquaries—British Archæological Association—Biblical Archæology—London and Middlesex Archæological Society—St. Paul's Ecclesiological Society—New Shakspere—Royal Society of Literature—Huguenot—The Odd Volumes—Anthropological Institute

OBITUARY MEMOIRS.—Mr. Francis Fry—Dr. Nicholson—Jin Jung Lung—Mr G T. Doo—Earl of Enniskillen—Mr G Smith.

REVIEWS of BOOKS —The Likeness of Christ—Life of Fuller—Society in the Elizabethan Age—Chapters from Family Chests—Life of Margaret of Navarre—Mythical Monsters—Account of the Guildhall—The Student's "Pickwick"

ANTIQUARIAN CORRESPONDENCE —The Late Bishop Hannington's Ancestry—A Reader of Curious Books—Throwing the Dart in Cork Harbour

GEORGE REDWAY, YORK STREET, COVENT GARDEN.

☞ THE ATHENÆUM says:—"Admirers of Thackeray may be grateful for a reprint of 'Sultan Stork.'"

In large 8vo, uniform with the New "Standard" Edition of Thackeray's Works. Price 10s. 6d.

Sultan Stork,

AND OTHER STORIES AND SKETCHES

BY

WILLIAM MAKEPEACE THACKERAY (1829—44).

Now first collected, to which is added the Bibliography of THACKERAY, revised and considerably enlarged.

CONTENTS.

INTRODUCTION
1. SULTAN STORK Being the One Thousand and Second Night By Major G O' G GAHAGAN. [1842.]
2. LITTLE SPITZ A Lenten Anecdote [1841]
3 DICKENS IN FRANCE An Account of a French dramatic version of "Nicholas Nickleby," performed at a Paris theatre [1842]
4. THE PARTIE FINE [1844]
5 ARABELLA; or, the Moral of the Partie Fine. [1844]
6 CARLYLE'S FRENCH REVOLUTION [1837.]
7 ELIZABETH BROWNRIGGE · A Tale. [1832]
8 AN EXHIBITION GOSSIP [1842]
9 LETTERS ON THE FINE ARTS. [1843]
10 CONTRIBUTIONS TO "THE SNOB"
11 CONTRIBUTIONS TO "THE NATIONAL STANDARD."
12 "DADDY, I'M HUNGRY." Scene in an Irish Coachmaker's Family.
[1843]

THE BIBLIOGRAPHY OF THACKERAY.
INDEX

GEORGE REDWAY, YORK STREET, COVENT GARDEN

In crown 8vo, cloth. Price 5s.

The History of Tithes.

BY

H. W. CLARKE, B.A,

GEORGE REDWAY, YORK STREET, COVENT GARDEN.

*In post 4to.   Illustrated with Engravings on Wood.   Most
chastely bound in white vellum.   Price 10s. 6d.*

ASTROLOGY THEOLOGIZED.

The Spiritual Hermeneutics of Astrology and Holy Writ.

BEING

*A Treatise upon the Influence of the Stars on Man,
and on the Art of Ruling them by the
Law of Grace.*

REPRINTED FROM THE ORIGINAL OF 1649

With a Prefatory Essay on Bible Hermeneutics.

BY

ANNA KINGSFORD, M.D., Paris.

———

"It is well for Dr. Anna Kingsford that she was not born into the sidereal world four hundred years ago   Had that been her sorry fate, she would assuredly have been burned at the stake for her preface to 'Astrology Theologised'   It is a very long preface—more than half the length of the treatise it introduces; it contains some of the finest flowers of Theosophical philosophy, and of course makes very short work of Christianity."—*St. James's Gazette.*

"Mrs. Kingsford, amid many things which we do not understand, and some few which we think we comprehend afar off, gives a more detailed analysis of ghosts than we remember to have met with in any of the ancient hermetic writers."—*St James's Gazette.*

"The only pleasing feature of the book are the reproductions of a number of beautiful symbolical figures with which it is illustrated   That on p 28, representing Christ surrounded by an elliptical glory and carried up to heaven by angels, is taken from an illuminated manuscript of the fourteenth century in the Bibliothèque Royale, and the figure of the Virgin in an aureole, on p 94, is from a tenth-century illuminated manuscript in the same library   Some of the figures here reproduced are among the finest things in Christian iconography "—*St. James's Gazette*

———

GEORGE REDWAY, YORK STREET, COVENT GARDEN

"The interest of this compilation is naturally not to be compared to that aroused by the ever fresh 'Thousand and One Nights;' but it has had high reputation among particular admirers, and the gentleman to whom we are indebted for this English version—apparently the most complete in any language of Western Europe—merits the thanks of the reading public for the work performed."—*Athenæum.*

About 500 pages, crown 8vo, cloth.   Price 10s. 6d.

The History of the Forty Vezirs;

OR,

The Story of the Forty Morns and Eves.

Written in Turkish by SHEYKH-ZADA, and now done into English by E. J. W. GIBB, M.R.A.S.

"A delightful addition to the wealth of Oriental stories available to English readers is 'The History of the Forty Vezirs' (Redway), done into English by Mr. E. J. W. Gibb, from the Turkish of Sheykh Zāda. The collection comprises 112 stories. To the forty told by the Lady and those of the forty Vezirs, Mr. Gibb has added four from Belletête, twenty from a MS. in the India Office, six from Dr. Behrnauer's translation, and two from a MS. recently purchased by Mr. Quaritch. The results of collation are admirably summarised in a comparative table that analyses the contents of the various texts. In the preface Mr. Gibb deals with the bibliography of the French and German versions, and indicates some of the more interesting parallels suggested by those old stories in the 'Gesta Romanorum,' the 'Decameron,' the 'Thousand and One Nights,' the 'Mabinogion,' and other treasures of old-world fable. In short, Mr. Gibb has considerately done everything to help the reader to an intelligent appreciation of this charming book."—*Saturday Review*

"In my opinion the version is definite and final. The style is light and pleasant with the absolutely necessary flavour of quaintness, and the notes, though short and few, are sufficient and satisfactory. Mr. Gibb does not write only *ad clerum;* and thus he has been obliged to 'leave in the obscurity of an Eastern language' three whole tales (pp 353, 366, and 399). No. 2 being exceedingly witty and fescennine. He has the good sense, when he supplants a broad joke by a *banal* English phrase, to subjoin in a note the original Turkish (pp 109, 140, 199, 215, and 382). Yet some of the *novelle* are highly spiced enough. see the amorous princess in the Eleventh Wazir's story (pp 381-3); and the truly Turkish and unspeakable version of modest Aesop's 'Countryman and his Son.' Of the less Milesian I would especially commend the story of the Venus-star and the magical angels, Harut and Marut (p. 167); the explanation of the proverb 'Take counsel of the cap that is on thy head' (p 362), and the Thirty-seventh Wazir's tale, showing why 'men have beaten their wives since the days of Saint Adam' (p. 349)—*Sir Richard F. Burton, in "The Academy"*

GEORGE REDWAY, YORK STREET, COVENT GARDEN

In demy 8vo, cloth. Price 10s. 6d.

The Mysteries of Magic;

A DIGEST OF

The Writings of Eliphas Levi.

WITH BIOGRAPHICAL AND CRITICAL ESSAY

BY

ARTHUR EDWARD WAITE.

Eliphas Levi, who died in 1865, and whose real name was Alphonse Louis Constant, ranks, beyond controversy, as the prince of the French adepts. His writings contain a revelation of the Grand Secret and a lucid interpretation of the theory of the Astral Light, which is the Great Magical Agent. His philosophy of miracles is of lasting value and interest, and absolutely indispensable to all students of occultism. It establishes a harmony between religion and science based on a rational explanation of all prodigies. Eliphas Levi revealed for the first time to the modern world the arcanum of will-power in the operations of transcendental magic, and he was also the originator of a new departure in Kabbalistic Exegesis. In the present digest, the information on the various branches of esoteric science, which is scattered over six large volumes of the French originals, has been diligently collated, and the translation carefully made

"A very curious book."—*Time.*

GEORGE REDWAY, YORK STREET, COVENT GARDEN.

In small 8vo, cloth. Price 5s.

Mountaineering Below the Snow-Line;

Or, the Solitary Pedestrian in Snowdonia and Elsewhere.

BY

M. PATERSON.

WITH ETCHINGS BY MACKANESS.

Vanity Fair says —"Mr. Paterson writes charmingly of a charming subject. He is a cultured and an athletic man, and tells of the climbs he has done in nervous, descriptive English He confesses to some partiality for getting along alone, but he is evidently not a churl, and he opens the store of his experiences under the snow-line in Wales, Cumberland, Scotland, and Norway with a skill which will make his wanderings acceptable to a much larger number of people than can ever climb mountains themselves"

GEORGE REDWAY, YORK STREET, COVENT GARDEN.

In demy 8vo, cloth, price 10s. 6d

Incidents in the Life of Madame Blavatsky,

Compiled from Information supplied by her Relatives and Friends,

AND EDITED BY

A. P. SINNETT.

With a Portrait reproduced from an Original Painting by HERMANN SCHMIECHEN.

"Mr Sinnett's memoir is fluently written, and is free from unsympathetic scepticism Theosophists will find both edification and interest in the book; and the general student of science will profit more or less by having his attention called to, &c. . . . ."—*Pall Mall Gazette.*

"Mr. Sinnett, however, offers on all the disputed points explanations which will be perfectly satisfactory to those who do not agree with the committee of the Psychical Society."—*Pall Mall Gazette*

"For any credulous friend who revels in such stories I can recommend 'Incidents in the Life of Madame Blavatsky' I READ EVERY LINE OF THE BOOK WITH MUCH INTEREST."—*Truth*

GEORGE REDWAY, YORK STREET, COVENT GARDEN

The Blood Covenant:

A Primitive Rite and its Bearings on Scripture.

BY

H. CLAY TRUMBULL, D.D.

Allusions to the shedding of blood as a pledge of friendship, or in connection with covenants, appear so frequently in literature and history that few can have failed to be impressed by them. Dr. Trumbull's book, however, will be a revelation to almost everyone. He shows that the rite was of almost universal observance in ancient times, and that it is so still among primitive people in every part of the world.

GEORGE REDWAY, YORK STREET, COVENT GARDEN.

In large crown 8vo, handsomely printed in borders with original headpieces, on a special make of toned paper, and bound in best cloth, the cover designed by MATHEW BELL. *Price 10s 6d.*

Sea Song and River Rhyme

From Chaucer to Tennyson.

SELECTED AND EDITED BY
ESTELLE DAVENPORT ADAMS.

With a New Poem by ALGERNON CHARLES SWINBURNE.
Illustrated with Etchings.

— —

"Mr Swinburne's new patriotic song, 'A Word for the Navy,' which will appear immediately in Mrs. Davenport Adams's anthology, 'Sea Song and River Rhyme,' is understood to be as fiery in its denunciation of those he believes to be antagonistic to the welfare of the country as was his lyric with which he startled the readers of the *Times* one morning "—*Athenæum*

GEORGE REDWAY, YORK STREET, COVENT GARDEN

In post 8vo, with numerous plates, coloured and plain, cloth.
Price 7s. 6d.

Geometrical Psychology;

OR,

The Science of Representation.

Being the Theories and Diagrams of B W BETTS

EXPLAINED BY
LOUISA S. COOK.

———

"His attempt (B. W. Betts') seems to have taken a similar direction to that of George Boole in logic, with the difference that, whereas Boole's expression of the Laws of Thought is algebraic, Betts expresses mind-growth geometrically, that is to say, his growth-formulæ are expressed in numerical series, of which each can be pictured to the eye in a corresponding curve. When the series are thus represented, they are found to resemble the forms of leaves and flowers."—*Extract from* "*Symbolic Methods of Study*," *by Mary Boole*

———

GEORGE REDWAY, YORK STREET, COVENT GARDEN.

A few copies only remain of the following important work, by the author of " The Rosicrucians."

Phallicism:

Its connexion with the Rosicrucians and the Gnostics, and its Foundation in Buddhism.

BY

HARGRAVE JENNINGS,

AUTHOR OF "THE ROSICRUCIANS."

Demy 8vo, cloth.

———

" This book is written *ad clerum*, and appeals to the scholar only, and not to the multitude. It is a masterly and exhaustive account of that worship of the creative powers of nature which, under various names, has prevailed among all the nations of antiquity and of mediæval times, alike in Egypt and India, in Italy and Gaul, among the Israelites of old, and among the primitive inhabitants of Great Britain and Ireland . . . . a most valuable auxiliary to all who care to pursue such a subject of inquiry, a subject for which Mr. Jennings is the better fitted on account of his long and intimate acquaintance with the Rosicrucians, their tenets, and their practices "—*Antiquarian Magazine and Bibliographer.*

" Unpleasant as this subject is, we are quite prepared to agree that in its scientific aspect, as a form of human worship, it has considerable importance. . . . . Mr. Jennings deals almost entirely with the subjective part of his enquiry, and he has evidently made a considerable amount of research into the literature of early religions. . . . He has produced something which is, at all events, worth the attention of the student of comparative psychology."—*Antiquary.*

" This book . . . is profoundly learned, and gives evidence on each page of deep thought, intense powers of research, clear and unmistakable reasoning, and thorough mastership of the subject. The appendix also contains much very curious matter which will interest those who desire to study the subject under all its different aspects and bearings."—*Reliquary*

———

GEORGE REDWAY, YORK STREET, COVENT GARDEN.

NEW NOVEL BY MR. A P. SINNETT,
Author of "Karma," &c.

In 2 vols., crown 8vo, cloth.
Published at 21s. Now offered at 10s. 6d.

United:

BY

A. P. SINNETT.

"Mr. Sinnett's previous works on 'Esoteric Buddhism' and 'The Occult World" in some way prepare the reader for the marvellous psychological phenomena with which the present volumes abound, and which cannot fail to have an irresistible charm for all those who love the byeways of speculation"
—*Literary World.*

"There is, nevertheless, a weird attractiveness about UNITED which makes even the non-believer in theosophy loth to put down the book when once he has taken it up, while to the lovers of occult phenomena it will prove irresistibly fascinating"—*Literary World.*

"Literary ability is evident throughout the book"—*St James's Gazette.*

"Mr Sinnett has produced a novel turning on psychic, mesmeric, and magnetic causes operating on English men and women of ordinary and very extraordinary types, and he has succeeded in making it of special interest for spiritualists and readable by common people"—*The Lady.*

"It is even doubtful whether Mr Sinnett will win one genuine convert to occultism by 'United,' but those who are occult already will take his powerful romance to their hearts, will pour out libations before him, and loudly cry well done."—*Court and Society Review*

"Over this thrice-silly subject the author has expended some most excellent writing, ideas that equal in breadth and strength some of those of our best writers, pure English, and undeniable grammar."—*The Whitehall Review*

GEORGE REDWAY, YORK STREET, COVENT GARDEN.

In preparation.

NEW TRANSLATION OF "THE HEPTAMERON."

The Heptameron;

OR,

Tales and Novels of Margaret, Queen of Navarre.

Now first done completely into English prose and verse, from the original French, by ARTHUR MACHEN.

GEORGE REDWAY, YORK STREET, COVENT GARDEN.

HINTS TO COLLECTORS

OF ORIGINAL EDITIONS OF

THE WORKS OF

William Makepeace Thackeray.

BY

CHARLES PLUMPTRE JOHNSON.

Printed on hand-made paper and bound in vellum.　Crown 8vo, 6s

The Edition is limited to five hundred and fifty copies,
twenty-five of which are on large paper.

———

" . . . A guide to those who are great admirers of Thackeray, and are collecting first editions of his works.　The dainty little volume, bound in parchment and printed on hand-made paper, is very concise and convenient in form; on each page is an exact copy of the title-page of the work mentioned thereon, a collation of pages and illustrations, useful hints on the differences in editions, with other matters indispensable to collectors . . Altogether it represents a large amount of labour and experience "—*The Spectator.*

" . . Mr Johnson has evidently done his work with so much loving care that we feel entire confidence in his statements.　The prices that he has affixed in every case form a valuable feature of the volume, which has been produced in a manner worthy of its subject matter "—*The Academy.*

" The list of works which Mr. Johnson supplies is likely to be of high interest to Thackeray collectors.　His preliminary remarks go beyond this not very narrow circle, and have a value for all collectors of modern works."— *Notes and Queries.*

" . . . It is choicely printed at the Chiswick Press; and the author, Mr. Charles Plumptre Johnson, treats the subject with evident knowledge and enthusiasm. . . .　It is not a Thackeray Bibliography, but a careful and minute description of the first issues, with full collations and statement of the probable cost . Mr Johnson addresses collectors, but is in addition a sincere admirer of the greatest satirist of the century."—*Book Lore.*

———

GEORGE REDWAY, YORK STREET, COVENT GARDEN.

HINTS TO COLLECTORS

OF ORIGINAL EDITIONS OF

THE WORKS OF

Charles Dickens.

BY

CHARLES PLUMPTRE JOHNSON.

Printed on hand-made paper, and bound in vellum.
Crown 8vo, 6s.

The Edition is limited to five hundred and fifty copies, fifty of which are on large paper.

"Enthusiastic admirers of Dickens are greatly beholden to Mr. C. P. Johnson for his useful and interesting 'Hints to Collectors of Original Editions of the Works of Charles Dickens' (Redway). The book is a companion to the similar guide to collectors of Thackeray's first editions, is compiled with the like care, and produced with the like finish and taste."— *The Saturday Review.*

"This is a sister volume to the 'Hints to Collectors of First Editions of Thackeray,' which we noticed a month or two ago. The works of Dickens with a few notable 'Dickensiana,' make up fifty-eight numbers . . . . and Mr. Johnson has further augmented the present volume with a list of thirty-six plays founded on Dickens's works, and another list of twenty-three published portraits of Dickens. As we are unable to detect any slips in his work, we must content ourselves with thanking him for the correctness of his annotations. It is unnecessary to repeat our praise of the elegant *format* of these books. . . . ."— *The Academy.*

GEORGE REDWAY, YORK STREET, COVENT GARDEN.

Just published, 32 pages, wrapper. Price 1s.

The New Illumination.

BY

EDWARD MAITLAND,

Author of "The Pilgrim and the Shrine."

GEORGE REDWAY, YORK STREET, COVENT GARDEN.

Handsomely printed and tastefully bound, 436 pages, large crown 8vo, cloth extra, 7s 6d

Essays in the Study of Folk-Songs.

BY THE

COUNTESS EVELYN MARTINENGO-CESARESCO.

"A pleasant volume on a pleasant topic. . . . The Countess, with her sincere enthusiasm for what is simple, passionate, and sensuous in folk-song, and with her lucid and unaffected style, well understands the mode in which the educated collector should approach the shy singers or story-tellers of Europe. . . . Her introduction is perhaps, to the scientific student of popular culture, the best part of her book . . . . Next to her introduction, perhaps her article on 'Death in Folk-Poetry' is the most serviceable essay in the volume. . . . . 'Folk Lullabies' is perhaps the most pleasant of the remaining essays in the admirable volume, a volume remarkable for knowledge, sympathy, and good taste."—Extracts from a page notice in the *Saturday Review*, April 24, 1886.

"This is a very delightful book, full of information and thoughtful suggestions. It deals principally with the Folk-songs of Southern peoples, Venetian, Sicilian, Armenian, Provence, and Greek Songs of Calabria, but there are several essays devoted to the general characteristics of Folk-Poetry, such as the influence of Nature, the Inspiration of Death, the idea of fate, the numerous songs connected with the rites of May, Folk-Lullabies, and Folk-Dirges. There is also an interesting essay on what is called the White Paternoster and Children's Rhyming Prayers. This is one of the most valuable, and certainly one of the most interesting, books which has been written on a subject which has of late years been exciting an ever-increasing attention, and which involves many important problems connected with the early history of the human race."—*Standard*.

"'Folk-Songs,' traditional popular ballads, are as tempting to me as King Charles's head to Mr. Dick. But interesting as the topic of the origin and diffusion and literary merit of these poems may be—poems much the same in all European countries—they are rather caviare to the general The Countess Martinengo-Cesaresco is, or should be, a well-known authority among special students of this branch of literature, to whom I heartily commend her 'Essays in the Study of Folk-Songs' The Countess is, perhaps, most familiar with Southern *volkslieder*, as of Greece, Italy, and Sicily. Her book is a treasure house of Folk-lore of various kinds, and the matter is handled with much poetic appreciation and a good deal of learning."—*Daily News*.

"A kind of popular introduction to the study of Folk-lore."—*St. James's Gazette*.

GEORGE REDWAY, YORK STREET, COVENT GARDEN.

In crown 8vo, in French grey wrapper. Price 6s.

A few copies on Large Paper. Price 10s. 6d.

The Bibliography of Swinburne;

A BIBLIOGRAPHICAL LIST, ARRANGED IN CHRONOLOGICAL ORDER, OF THE PUBLISHED WRITINGS IN VERSE AND PROSE

OF

ALGERNON CHARLES SWINBURNE
(1857-1884).

This Bibliography commences with the brief-lived College Magazine, to which Mr SWINBURNE was one of the chief contributors when an undergraduate at Oxford in 1857-8. Besides a careful enumeration and description of the first editions of all his separately published volumes and pamphlets in verse and prose, the original appearance is duly noted of every poem, prose article, or letter, contributed to any journal or magazine (e g., *Once a Week*, *The Spectator*, *The Cornhill Magazine*, *The Morning Star*, *The Fortnightly Review*, *The Examiner*, *The Dark Blue*, *The Academy*, *The Athenæum*, *The Tatler*, *Belgravia*, *The Gentleman's Magazine*, *La République des Lettres*, *Le Rappel*, *The Glasgow University Magazine*, *The Daily Telegraph*, &c., &c), whether collected or uncollected Among other entries will be found a remarkable novel, published in instalments, and never issued in a separate form, and several productions in verse not generally known to be from Mr SWINBURNE s pen The whole forms a copious and it is believed approximately complete record of a remarkable and brilliant literary career, extending already over a quarter of a century.

** ONLY 250 COPIES PRINTED.

GEORGE REDWAY, YORK STREET, COVENT GARDEN.

Post free, price 3d.

The Literature of Occultism and Archæology.

Being a Catalogue of Books ON SALE relating to

Ancient Worships.
Astrology.
Alchemy.
Animal Magnetism.
Anthropology
Arabic.
Assassins.
Antiquities.
Ancient History.
Behmen and the Mystics.
Buddhism.
Clairvoyance.
Cabeiri.
China
Coins.
Druids.
Dreams and Visions.
Divination.
Divining Rod.
Demonology.
Ethnology.
Egypt.
Fascination.
Flagellants.
Freemasonry.
Folk-Lore.
Gnostics.
Gems.
Ghosts.
Hindus.   [Writing.
Hieroglyphics and Secret
Herbals.
Hermetic.
India and the Hindus.
Kabbala
Koran
Miracles.
Mirabilaries

Magic and Magicians.
Mysteries
Mithraic Worship.
Mesmerism.
Mythology.
Metaphysics.
Mysticism.
Neo-platonism.
Orientalia
Obelisks.
Oracles.
Occult Sciences.
Philology.
Persian.
Parsees.
Philosophy
Physiognomy.
Palmistry and Handwriting.
Phrenology.
Psychoneurology.
Psychometry.
Prophets.
Rosicrucians.
Round Towers.
Rabbinical.
Spiritualism.   [and Quakers.
Skeptics, Jesuits, Christians,
Sibylls.
Symbolism.
Serpent Worship
Secret Societies.
Somnambulism
Travels
Tombs.
Theosophical
Theology and Criticism.
Witchcraft.

GEORGE REDWAY, YORK STREET, COVENT GARDEN

In crown 8vo, cloth.   Price 7s. 6d.

Theosophy, Religion, and Occult Science.

BY

HENRY S. OLCOTT,

PRESIDENT OF THE THEOSOPHICAL SOCIETY.

WITH GLOSSARY OF INDIAN TERMS AND INDEX.

"This book, to which we can only allot an amount of space quite incommensurate with its intrinsic interest, is one that will appeal to the prepared student rather than to the general reader. To any one who has previously made the acquaintance of such books as Mr. Sinnett's 'Occult World,' and 'Esoteric Buddhism,' or has in other ways familiarised himself with the doctrines of the so-called Theosophical Society or Brotherhood, these lectures of Colonel Olcott's will be rich in interest and suggestiveness. The American officer is a person of undoubted social position and unblemished personal reputation, and his main object is not to secure belief in the reality of any 'phenomena,' not to win a barren reputation for himself as a thaumaturgist or wonder-worker, but to win acceptance for one of the oldest philosophies of nature and human life—a philosophy to which of late years the thinkers of the West have been turning with noteworthy curiosity and interest. Of course, should the genuineness of the phenomena in question be satisfactorily established, there would undoubtedly be proof that the Eastern sages to whom Colonel Olcott bears witness do possess a knowledge of the laws of the physical universe far wider and more intimate than that which has been laboriously acquired by the inductive science of the West; but the theosophy expounded in this volume is at once a theology, a metaphysic, and a sociology, in which mere marvels, as such, occupy a quite subordinate and unimportant position. We cannot now discuss its claims, and we will not pronounce any opinion upon them, we will only say that Colonel Olcott's volume deserves and will repay the study of all readers for whom the bye-ways of speculation have an irresistible charm."—*Manchester Examiner.*

GEORGE REDWAY, YORK STREET, COVENT GARDEN.

Now ready, at all Booksellers', and at Smith's Railway Bookstalls.
Popular Edition, price 2s. 6d.

Burma:

AS IT WAS, AS IT IS, AND AS IT WILL BE

BY

J. G SCOTT ("Shway Yoe").

Crown 8vo, cloth

" Before going to help to govern them, Mr. Scott has once more written on the Burmese . . . Mr Scott claims to have covered the whole ground, to show Burma as it was, is, and will be, and as there is nobody competent to criticise him except himself, we shall not presume to say how far he has succeeded. What, however, may be asserted with absolute confidence is, that he has written a bright, readable, and useful book."—*Saturday Review*, March 27.

" Very lively and readable "—*Pall Mall Gazette*

" The author knows what he writes about."—*St Stephen's Review.*

" There is a good deal of curious reading in the book."—*Literary World.*

" The book is amusing and instructing, and Mr. George Redway, the publisher, will have done the public and himself a service."—*Court Journal.*

" The print is clear, and the binding in excellent taste."—*Bookseller.*

" Evidently full of genuine information "—*Society.*

" A handy guide to Burma, as readable as it is accurate "—*Globe.*

" Mr Scott should have called this volume ' A book for Members of Parliament ' "—*London and China Telegraph.*

" The sketch of Burmese cosmogony and mythology is very interesting."—*Nature.*

" A competent historian He sketches Burma and the Burmans with minute fidelity."—*Daily Chronicle*

" Probably no Englishman knows Burma better than Mr. J. G Scott "—*Contemporary Review*

" An excellent description both of land and people "—*Contemporary Review*

" Most interesting."—*St. James's Gazette*

" Shway Yoe is a graphic writer . no one can supply this information better than Mr. Scott "—*Asiatic Quarterly Review*

GEORGE REDWAY YORK STREET, COVENT GARDEN

A few large paper copies, with India proof portrait, in imperial 8vo, parchment paper covers. Price 7s. 6d

An
Essay on the Genius of George Cruikshank

BY

"THETA" (WILLIAM MAKEPEACE THACKERAY).

With all the Original Woodcut Illustrations, a New Portrait of CRUIKSHANK etched by PAILTHORPE, and a Prefatory Note on THACKERAY AS AN ART CRITIC by W. E. CHURCH.

"Thackeray's essay 'On the Genius of George Cruikshank,' reprinted from the *Westminster Review*, is a piece of work well calculated to drive a critic of these days to despair How inimitable is its touch ! At once familiar and elegant, serious and humorous, enthusiastically appreciative, and yet just and clear sighted, but above all, what the French call *personnel* It is not the impersonnel reviewer who is going through his paces . . . it is Thackeray talking to us as few can talk—talking with apparent carelessness, even ramblingly, but never losing the thread of his discourse or saying a word too much, nor ever missing a point which may help to elucidate his subject or enhance the charm of his essay. . . . . Mr. W. E. Church's prefatory note on 'Thackeray as an Art Critic' is interesting and carefully compiled."—*Westminster Review*, Jan 15th

"As the original copy of the *Westminster* is now excessively rare, this re-issue will, no doubt, be welcomed by collectors."—*Birmingham Daily Mail*

"The new portrait of Cruikshank by F. W. Pailthorpe is a clear, firm etching"—*The Artist*.

GEORGE REDWAY, YORK STREET, COVENT GARDEN.

In demy 8vo, wrapper, uncut, with Extra Portrait. Price 5s.

"Phiz" (Hablot Knight Browne) :

A Memoir ; including a Selection from his Correspondence and Notes on his Principal Works. By FRED. G. KITTON.

With a Portrait and numerous Illustrations.

☞ *A few copies only remain.*

GEORGE REDWAY, YORK STREET, COVENT GARDEN.

Issued Monthly.   Annual subscription, payable in advance, 5s.

The East Anglian;

OR,

Notes and Queries

ON SUBJECTS CONNECTED WITH THE COUNTIES OF SUFFOLK
CAMBRIDGE, ESSEX, AND NORFOLK.

EDITED BY THE
Rev. C. H EVELYN WHITE, F.R.Hist.S.

" Antiquities are history defaced, or remnants that have escaped the ship-
wreck of time . . . . wrecks of history wherein the memory of things is almost
lost; or such particulars as industrious persons, with exact and scrupulous
diligence can anyway collect from genealogies, calendars, titles, inscriptions,
monuments, coins, names, etymologies, proverbs, traditions, archives, instruments fragments of private and public history, scattered passages, of books no
way historical, &c, by which means something is recovered from the deluge of
time . . .   In this imperfect history no deficiency need be noted, it being of
its own nature imperfect."—*LORD BACON, Advancement of Learning.*

GEORGE REDWAY, YORK STREET, COVENT GARDEN.

---

1 vol., crown 8vo, 400 pages, cloth, 6s.

A Regular Pickle:

How He Sowed his Wild Oats.

BY
HENRY W. NESFIELD,
Author of " A Chequered Career."

" Mr. Nesfield's name as an author is established on such a pleasantly sound
foundation that it is a recognised fact that, in taking up a book written by him,
the reader is in for a delightful half-hour, during which his risible and humour-
ous faculties will be pleasantly stimulated   The history of young Archibald
Highton Tregauntly, whose fortunes we follow from the cradle to when experience is just beginning to teach him a few wholesome lessons, is as smart and
brisk as it is possible to be."—*Whitehall Review*

" It will be matter for regret if the brisk and lively style of Mr Nesfield,
who at times reminds us of LEVER, should blind people to the downright
wickedness of such a perverted career as is here described."—*Daily Chronicle.*

GEORGE REDWAY, YORK STREET, COVENT GARDEN.

544 pages, crown 8vo, green cloth boards, price 7s. 6d. (Only 500 copies printed.)

Dickensiana.

A Bibliography of the Literature relating to CHARLES DICKENS and his Writings

Compiled by FRED. G. KITTON, author of "'Phiz' (Hablôt K. Browne), a Memoir," and "John Leech, Artist and Humourist." With a Portrait of "Boz," from a Drawing by SAMUEL LAURENCE

"This book is honestly what it pretends to be, and nothing more. It is a comprehensive catalogue of all the writings of Mr. Charles Dickens, and of a good quantity of books written about him   It also contains copious extracts from reviews of his works and from sermons on his character. The criticisms are so various, and some of them are so much at variance with others, that the reader of them can complain of nothing less than a lack of material on which to form his judgment, if he has not formed it already, on the claim of Mr. Dickens to occupy a front place in the rank of English classics   Assertions, if not arguments, are multiplied on either side "—*Saturday Review*

"Mr. Fred. G Kitton . . . has done his work with remarkable thoroughness, and consequently with real success   It is a subject on which I may fairly claim to speak, and I may say that all that I know, and a great deal I did not know, about Dickens is to be found in Mr Kitton's work "—"*Atlas*," in the *World*.

" DICKENSIANA "

" If, with your Dickens-lore you'd make
 Considerable headway,
The way to be well-read 's to take
 This book brought out by REDWAY.
'Tis clear, exhaustive, and compact,
 Both well-arranged and written,
A mine of anecdote and fact,
 Compiled by F G KITTON "—*Punch*

GEORGE REDWAY, YORK STREET, COVENT GARDEN

In the press.

MR. SWINBURNE'S NEW POEM.

A Word for the Navy.

BY

ALGERNON CHARLES SWINBURNE.

Edition limited to 250 copies, each numbered.

GEORGE REDWAY, YORK STREET, COVENT GARDEN.

Transactions of the London Lodge of the Theosophical Society:

Nos. 1 and 2.—Out of print.

No. 3.—On the Higher Aspect of Theosophic Studies. By MOHINI M. CHATTERJI.

No. 4.—A Synopsis of Baron Du Prel's "Philosophie der Mystik." By BERTRAM KEIGHTLEY.

No. 5.—A Paper on Reincarnation. By MISS ARUNDALE. And other Proceedings.

No 6.—The Theosophical Movement. By A. P. SINNETT.

No. 7.—The Higher Self. By A. P. SINNETT.

No. 8.—The Theosophical Society and its Work. By MOHINI M. CHATTERJI.

No. 9.—A Paper on Krishna. By MOHINI M CHATTERJI.

No. 10.—On Mesmerism. By A. P. SINNETT.

No. 11.—Theosophy in the Works of Richard Wagner. By W. ASHTON ELLIS.

Nos. 3 to 11, and each succeeding number as issued, may be had, price One Shilling

GEORGE REDWAY, YORK STREET, COVENT GARDEN.

In large crown 8vo. Price 3s. 6d.

Sithron, the Star Stricken.

Translated (*Ala bereket Allah*) from an ancient Arabic Manuscript.

BY

SALEM BEN UZAIR, of Bassora.

"This very remarkable book, 'Sithron,' . . is a bold, pungent, audacious satire upon the ancient religious belief of the Jews . No one can read the book without homage to the force, the tenderness, and the never-failing skill of its writer."—*St James's Gazette*

GEORGE REDWAY, YORK STREET, COVENT GARDEN.

In demy 8vo, choicely printed, and bound in Japanese parchment.
Price 7s. 6d.

Primitive Symbolism

As Illustrated in Phallic Worship; or, the Reproductive
Principle.

BY

The late HODDER M. WESTROPP.

With an Introduction by MAJOR-GENERAL FORLONG, Author of
" Rivers of Life."

" This work is a *multum in parvo* of the growth and spread of Phallicism,
as we commonly call the worship of nature or fertilizing powers   I felt, when
solicited to enlarge and illustrate it on the sudden death of the lamented
author, that it would be desecration to touch so complete a compendium by
one of the most competent and soundest thinkers who have written on this
world-wide faith   None knew better or saw more clearly than Mr. Westropp
that in this oldest symbolism and worship lay the foundations of all the goodly
systems we call Religions "—J. G. R FORLONG.

" A well-selected repertory of facts illustrating this subject, which should
be read by all who are interested in the study of the growth of religions "—
Westminster Review.

GEORGE REDWAY, YORK STREET, COVENT GARDEN.

In imperial 16mo, on Dutch paper, cloth extra.   Price 2s. 6d.

The Rueing of Gudrun,

And other Poems.

BY THE

Hon. Mrs. GREVILLE-NUGENT.

" It is clear from many exquisite passages that Mrs Nugent, if she were
so minded and in earnest, might be a real poetess "—*Daily Telegraph*

" The writer touches the various chords of her lyre with no inexperienced
hand."—*Morning Post.*

" Mrs. Greville-Nugent has succeeded very fairly well with her villanelles
and rondeaux, her triolets and sestines, her ballades and chants royal "—
St James's Gazette

" Where she shows herself at her best is in the French forms of verse,
which exactly suit her talent "—*The Times.*

GEORGE REDWAY, YORK STREET, COVENT GARDEN.

In small 8vo, handsomely printed on antique paper, and tastefully bound. Price 2s. 6d.

Pope Joan

(*THE FEMALE POPE*).

A Historical Study. Translated from the Greek of Emmanuel Rhoidis, with Preface by

CHARLES HASTINGS COLLETTE.

———

"When Dr. Dollinger wrote to the effect that 'the subject of Pope Joan has not yet lost interest,' he said no more than the truth   The probability is that the topic will always have its attractions for the lovers of the curiosities of history. Mr Baring-Gould has declared that 'the whole story of Pope Joan is fabulous, and rests on not a single historical foundation,' but others are not so firmly convinced in the matter, and at all times there are those who are anxious to investigate singular traditions. To the two latter classes the little monograph on 'Pope Joan,' written by Emmanuel Rhoidis, edited with a preface by Mr C H Collette, and published by Mr. Redway, will be very acceptable   The author discusses the topic with much learning and ingenuity, and Mr Collette's introduction is full of information"—*Globe*

GEORGE REDWAY, YORK STREET, COVENT GARDEN.

In 2 vols., cloth, 6s.

The Curate's Wife.

A Story of Country Life.

BY

J. E. PANTON.

"The author of "Less Than Kin" has produced in "The Curate's Wife" a story as powerful and full of genuine human interest as has appeared for some long time past   This tale of "country life" is realistic in the best sense of the word   Faithful as a photograph in all its minor details, it shows clear insight into character of both the sexes, and under very varied conditions. It would have been, doubtless, more satisfactory had Meta conquered in the unequal contest between her well-meaning inexperience and her husband's brutal self-love, but in real life the chances would be against her, and this clever novel is, above all, an exact picture of certain phases of human nature as it is, and in this lies its chief merit."—*Morning Post*, May 19th, 1886.

GEORGE REDWAY, YORK STREET, COVENT GARDEN.

Demy 18mo, 200 pages, cloth, uncut   Price 2s

Wellerisms

FROM

"*Pickwick*" and "*Master Humphrey's Clock.*"

Selected by CHARLES F. RIDEAL.

EDITED, WITH AN INTRODUCTION,

BY

CHARLES KENT,

AUTHOR OF "THE HUMOUR AND PATHOS OF CHARLES DICKENS"

"Some write well, but he writes Weller."—*Epigram on Dickens*

"Some of the best sayings of the immortal Sam and his sportive parent are collected here   The book may be taken up for a few minutes with the certainty of affording amusement, and it can be carried away in the pocket."—*Literary World.*

"It was a very good idea . . . . the extracts are very humorous . . . . here nothing is missed "—*Glasgow Herald.*

GEORGE REDWAY, YORK STREET, COVENT GARDEN.

Sphinx:

Monatsschrift fur die geschichtliche und experimentale Begründung der ubersinnlichen Weltanschauung auf monistischer Grundlage herausgegeben von HUBBE SCHLEIDEN, Dr. J. U.

1s 6d. monthly; 12s. per annum

"We cordially recommend this magazine to all those of our readers who are acquainted with the German language, as it promises to be one of the best extant periodicals treating of transcendental subjects."—*The Theosophist*

GEORGE REDWAY, YORK STREET, COVENT GARDEN.

In crown 8vo, 2 vols., cloth   Price 6s

The Valley of Sorek.

BY

GERTRUDE M. GEORGE.

With a Critical Introduction by RICHARD HERNE SHEPHERD.

"There is in the book a high and pure moral and a distinct conception of character . . . The *dramatis personæ* . . . are in reality strongly individual, and surprise one with their inconsistencies just as real human beings do . . There is something powerful in the way in which the reader is made to feel both the reality and the untrustworthiness of his [the hero's] religious fervour, and the character of the atheist, Graham, is not less strongly and definitely conceived . . . It is a work that shows imagination and moral insight, and we shall look with much anticipation for another from the same hand "—*Contemporary Review.*

GEORGE REDWAY, YORK STREET, COVENT GARDEN.

Price 1s.

Low Down :

Wayside Thoughts in Ballad and other Verse.

BY

TWO TRAMPS.

"This is a collection of short pieces, most of which can fairly be considered poetry—no slight merit, as verses run just now. Some of the pieces are singularly pathetic and mournful, others, though in serious guise, are permeated by quaint humour, and all of them are of considerable merit From the variety and excellence of the contents of this bundle of poetical effusions, it is likely to attract a great number of readers, and many passages in it are particularly suitable for recitation "—*Army and Navy Gazette*, Aug 14, 1886.

"But 'Low Down,' as it is called, has the distinction of being multi-coloured, each sheet of eight pages consisting of paper of a special hue. To turn over the leaves is, in fact, to enjoy a sort of kaleidoscopic effect, a glimpse of a literary rainbow. Moreover, to complete the peculiarity of the thing, the various poems are printed, apparently at haphazard, in large or small type, as the case may be There are those, perhaps, who would take such jokes too seriously, and bring them solemnly to the bar of taste, there to be as solemnly condemned But that is scarcely the right spirit in which to regard them There is room in life for the quaint and curious as well as for the neat and elegant "—*The Globe.*

GEORGE REDWAY, YORK STREET, COVENT GARDEN

In crown 8vo, parchment.   *Price 3s. 6d.*

The
Anatomy of Tobacco;

Or, Smoking Methodised, Divided and Considered after
a New Fashion.

BY

LEOLINUS SILURIENSIS.

"A very clever and amusing parody of the metaphysical treatises once in fashion. Every smoker will be pleased with this volume."—*Notes and Queries.*

"We have here a most excellent piece of fooling, evidently from a University pen . . contains some very clever burlesques of classical modes of writing, and a delicious parody of scholastic logic."—*Literary World*

"A delightful mock essay on the exoteric philosophy of the pipe and the pipe bowl . . . reminding one alternately of 'Melancholy' Burton and Herr Teufelsdröch, and implying vast reading and out-of-the-way culture on the part of the author."—*Bookseller.*

GEORGE REDWAY, YORK STREET, COVENT GARDEN.

NEW REALISTIC NOVEL.

---

620 pages, handsomely bound.   *Price 6s.*

Leicester:
AN AUTOBIOGRAPHY.

BY

FRANCIS W. L. ADAMS.

"Even M. Zola and Mr. George Moore would find it hard to beat Mr. Adams's description of Rosy's death. The grimly minute narrative of Leicester's schoolboy troubles and of his attempt to get a living when he is discarded by his guardian is, too, of such a character as to make one regret that Mr. Adams had not put to better use his undoubted, though undisciplined, powers."—*The Academy.*

"There is unquestionable power in 'Leicester.'"—*The Athenæum.*

GEORGE REDWAY, YORK STREET, COVENT GARDEN.

EBENEZER JONES'S POEMS

In post 8vo, cloth, old style   Price 5s.

Studies of Sensation and Event.

Poems by EBENEZER JONES.

Edited, Prefaced, and Annotated by RICHARD HERNE SHEPHERD.

With Memorial Notices of the Author by SUMNER JONES
and W. J. LINTON.

A new Edition.   With Photographic Portrait of the Poet.

"This remarkable poet affords nearly the most striking instance of neglected genius in our modern school of poetry.   His poems are full of vivid disorderly power."—D. G ROSSETTI

GEORGE REDWAY, YORK STREET, COVENT GARDEN.

In demy 8vo, elegantly printed on Dutch hand-made paper, and bound in parchment-paper cover   Price 1s.

The Scope and Charm of Antiquarian Study.

BY

JOHN BATTY, F.R.Hist.S.,

MEMBER OF THE YORKSHIRE ARCHÆOLOGICAL AND TOPOGRAPHICAL ASSOCIATION.

"It forms a useful and entertaining guide to a beginner in historical researches."—*Notes and Queries*

"The author has laid it before the public in a most inviting, intelligent, and intelligible form, and offers every incentive to the study in every department, including Ancient Records, Manorial Court-Rolls, Heraldry, Painted Glass, Mural Paintings, Pottery, Church Bells, Numismatics, Folk-Lore, &c , to each of which the attention of the student is directed   The pamphlet is printed on a beautiful modern antique paper, appropriate to the subject of the work "—*Brighton Examiner.*

"Mr. Batty, who is one of those folks Mr Dobson styles 'gleaners after time,' has clearly and concisely summed up, in the space of a few pages, all the various objects which may legitimately be considered to come within the scope of antiquarian study."—*Academy*

GEORGE REDWAY, YORK STREET, COVENT GARDEN.

An édition de luxe, in demy 18mo.   Price 1s.

Confessions of an English Hachish Eater.

"There is a sort of bizarre attraction in this fantastic little book, with its weird, unhealthy imaginations "—*Whitehall Review.*

"Imagination or some other faculty plays marvellous freaks in this little book."—*Lloyd's Weekly.*

"A weird little book   . .   The author seems to have been delighted with his dreams, and .   .   carefully explains how hachish may be made from the resin of the common hemp plant."—*Daily Chronicle*

"To be added to the literature of what is, after all, a very undesirable subject.   Weak minds may generate a morbid curiosity if stimulated in this direction."—*Bradford Observer*

"The stories told by our author have a decidedly Oriental flavour, and we would not be surprised if some foolish individuals did endeavour to procure some of the drug, with a view to experience the sensation described by the writer of this clever *brochure*"—*Edinburgh Courant*

GEORGE REDWAY, YORK STREET, COVENT GARDEN

NEWLY-DISCOVERED POEM BY CHARLES LAMB.

Beauty and the Beast;

OR,

A Rough Outside with a Gentle Heart.

By CHARLES LAMB. Now first reprinted from the Original Edition of 1811, with Preface and Notes

BY

RICHARD HERNE SHEPHERD.

ONLY 100 COPIES PRINTED.

Fcap. 8vo, printed on handsome paper at the Chiswick Press, and bound in parchment by Burn to form a companion volume to "Tamerlane." Price 10s. 6d.

GEORGE REDWAY, YORK STREET, COVENT GARDEN

THE ONLY PUBLISHED BIOGRAPHY OF JOHN LEECH.

———

An édition de luxe in demy 18mo.   Price 1s.

John Leech,

ARTIST AND HUMOURIST.

A BIOGRAPHICAL SKETCH.

BY

FRED. G. KITTON.

New Edition, revised.

———

"In the absence of a fuller biography we cordially welcome Mr. Kitton's interesting little sketch."—*Notes and Queries*

"The multitudinous admirers of the famous artist will find this touching monograph well worth careful reading and preservation."—*Daily Chronicle.*

"The very model of what such a memoir should be"—*Graphic.*

GEORGE REDWAY, YORK STREET, COVENT GARDEN.

———

Fourth Edition, newly revised, in demy 8vo, with Illustrative Plates.

Price 1s.

The Handbook of Palmistry,

BY

ROSA BAUGHAN,

AUTHOR OF "INDICATIONS OF CHARACTER IN HANDWRITING"

"It possesses a certain literary interest, for Miss Baughan shows the connection between palmistry and the doctrines of the Kabbala."—*Graphic*

"Miss Rosa Baughan, for many years known as one of the most expert proficients in this branch of science, has as much claim to consideration as any writer on the subject"—*Sussex Daily News*

"People who wish to believe in palmistry, or the science of reading character from the marks of the hand," says the *Daily News*, in an article devoted to the discussion of this topic, "will be interested in a handbook of the subject by Miss Baughan, published by Mr. Redway"

GEORGE REDWAY, YORK STREET, COVENT GARDEN.

Fourth Edition.   With Engraved Frontispiece.   In crown 8vo, 5s.

Cosmo de' Medici;
An Historical Tragedy.   And other Poems.

BY

RICHARD HENGIST HORNE,
Author of " Orion "

" This tragedy is the work of a poet and not of a playwright   Many of the scenes abound in vigour and tragic intensity   If the structure of the drama challenges comparison with the masterpieces of the Elizabethan stage, it is at least not unworthy of the models which have inspired it."—*Times*

GEORGE REDWAY, YORK STREET, COVENT GARDEN.

Edition limited to 500 copies, handsomely printed on antique paper and tastefully bound.   Price 7s. 6d

THE ASTROLOGER'S GUIDE.

Anima Astrologiae;
OR, A
Guide for Astrologers.

Being the One Hundred and Forty-six Considerations of the Astrologer, GUIDO BONATUS, translated from the Latin by Henry Coley, together with the choicest Aphorisms of the Seven Segments of JEROM CARDAN, of Milan, edited by William Lilly (1675), now first republished from the original edition with Notes and Preface

BY

W. C. ELDON SERJEANT.

" Mr. Serjeant deserves the thanks of all who are interested in astrology for rescuing this important work from oblivion   . The growing interest in mystical science will lead to a revival of astrological study, and advanced students will find this book an indispensable addition to their libraries.   The book is well got up and printed "—*Theosophist*

GEORGE REDWAY, YORK STREET, COVENT GARDEN.

FIFTH THOUSAND
An édition de luxe in demy 18mo
Bound in fancy cloth, uncut edges. Price 2s.

Tobacco Talk and Smokers' Gossip.

An Amusing Miscellany of Fact and Anecdote relating to
"The Great Plant" in all its Forms and Uses, including
a Selection from Nicotian Literature.

"One of the best books of gossip we have met for some time. . . It is literally crammed full from beginning to end of its 148 pages with well-selected anecdotes, poems, and excerpts from tobacco literature and history."—*Graphic.*

"The smoker should be grateful to the compilers of this pretty little volume . . . . No smoker should be without it, and anti-tobacconists have only to turn over its leaves to be converted."—*Pall Mall Gazette*

"Something to please smokers; and non-smokers may be interested in tracing the effect of tobacco—the fatal, fragrant herb—on our literature."—*Literary World.*

GEORGE REDWAY, YORK STREET, COVENT GARDEN.

The
Handbook of Physiognomy.
BY
ROSA BAUGHAN.

Demy 8vo, wrapper, 1s.

"The merit of her book consists in the admirable clearness of her descriptions of faces So vivid is the impression produced by them that she is able to dispense with illustrations, the reader using the faces of his acquaintances for that purpose. The classification, too, is good, although the astrological headings may be regarded by the profane as fanciful Physiognomy may now be scientifically studied by means of composite photography."—*Pall Mall Gazette.*

GEORGE REDWAY, YORK STREET, COVENT GARDEN.

In preparation.

Price to Subscribers, 6s.

The Praise of Ale;

OR,

Songs, Ballads, Epigrams, and Anecdotes relating to

Beer, Malt, and Hops.

Collected and arranged by

W. T. MARCHANT.

CONTENTS.—Introduction; History; Carols and Wassail Songs, Church Ales and Observances, Whitsun Ales; Political, Harvest; General, Barley and Malt; Hops; Scotch Songs; Local and Dialect; Trade Songs, Oxford Songs; Ale Wives, Brewers, Drinking Clubs and Customs, Royal and Noble Drinkers; Black Beer, Drinking Vessels, Warm Ale; Facts, Scraps, and Ana, Index.

The volume will contain much curious and out-of-the-way information, embracing a short sketch of the rise and progress of the art of brewing in this country, an account of the laws relating to beer, and the statutes against drunkenness, of the manners and customs of "malt worms" and mug-house clubs, and the obsolete phraseology of "toss-pots," such as "super-nagulum," "upsee-freeze," "shoeing horns," and "carousing the hunter's hoop." The author will pay attention to the drinking customs more or less connected with the Church—Whitsun Ales, Bride Ales, Bride Bush, Bride Wain, and the like, the chants of the wassail-bowl, of the Hock Cart, and the Sheepshearing and Harvest Home rejoicings—

> " Here's a health to the Barley mow, brave boys,
> Here's a health to the Barley mow"—

and Brazenose songs in honour of the brew for which that college is renowned Then there are lyrics pertaining to particular sorts and conditions of men, as the songs of the threshers and tinkers, sailors and soldiers, and the clubs, which may be considered as forming a class of themselves This work will doubtless prove a valuable and pleasant addition to the library of the student of history and lover of poetry

GEORGE REDWAY, YORK STREET, COVENT GARDEN.

In preparation.

THE PLAYS OF GEORGE COLMAN THE YOUNGER.

The Comedies and Farces

OF

GEORGE COLMAN THE YOUNGER.

Now first collected and carefully reprinted from the Original Editions, with Annotations and Critical and Bibliographical Preface,

BY

RICHARD HERNE SHEPHERD.

In Two Volumes.

"Mr. R. H Shepherd is engaged in collecting and reprinting, with a critical and biographical introduction and annotations, the dramatic works of George Colman the younger, which will shortly be published in two volumes by Mr. Redway, of York Street Most of them were issued in Colman's lifetime in pamphlet form, but many have, nevertheless, become scarce, and of those which, like the 'Heir-at-Law,' 'John Bull,' and 'The Poor Gentleman' have held the stage, the text has become more or less corrupted Considering the great popularity of Colman's plays, the spirit and humour of their scenes and their association with the names of great actors in the past, it is a curious fact that Mr. Shepherd's publication, though it appears more than a century after the production of the earliest of Colman's pieces on the stage, will be the first collected edition. It will comprise, of course, the suppressed preface to 'The Iron Chest,' in which Colman made his famous personal attack upon John Kemble."—*Daily News.*

GEORGE REDWAY, YORK STREET, COVENT GARDEN.

To be published shortly, handsomely printed and bound in one vol.
Small demy 8vo, price 10s. 6d.

The Kabala Denudata

(Translated into English),

CONTAINING THE FOLLOWING BOOKS OF THE ZOHAR —

1. *The Book of Concealed Mystery.*
2. *The Greater Holy Assembly.*
3. *The Lesser Holy Assembly.*

Collated with the original Hebrew and the Latin text of Knorr
de Rosenroth's " Kabala Denudata,"

BY

S. LIDDELL MACGREGOR MATHERS.

GEORGE REDWAY, YORK STREET, COVENT GARDEN

---

64 pp., 8vo, wrapper.   Price 1s. 6d.

The

" Occult   World   Phenomena "

AND

The Society for Psychical Research.

BY

A. P. SINNETT,

AUTHOR OF " THE OCCULT WORLD," " ESOTERIC BUDDHISM," ETC.

With a Protest by MADAME BLAVATSKY.

———

" An interesting addition to the fast-expanding literature of Theosophy."
—*Literary World*

" All who are interested in Theosophy should read it."—*Glasgow Herald.*

" Mr Sinnett scores some points against his adversary, and his pamphlet
is to be followed by some memoirs of Madame Blavatsky, which may contain
further refutations.   Madame Blavatsky herself appends to the pamphlet a
brief and indignant denial of the grave charges which have been made against
her."—*Graphic*

GEORGE REDWAY, YORK STREET, COVENT GARDEN.

Small 4to, with Illustrations, bound in vegetable parchment.
Price 10s. 6d.

The Virgin of the World.

BY

HERMES MERCURIUS TRISMEGISTUS.

A Treatise on INITIATIONS. or ASCLEPIOS; the DEFI-
NITIONS of ASCLEPIOS; FRAGMENTS of the
WRITINGS OF HERMES

TRANSLATED AND EDITED BY THE AUTHORS OF "THE PERFECT
WAY"

With an introduction to "The Virgin of the World" by A. K.,
and an Essay on "The Hermetic Books" by E. M.

"It will be a most interesting study for every occultist to compare the
doctrines of the ancient Hermetic philosophy with the teaching of the Vedantic
and Buddhist systems of religious thought. The famous books of Hermes
seem to occupy, with reference to the Egyptian religion, the same position
which the Upanishads occupy in Aryan religious literature"—*The Theosophist*,
November, 1885.

GEORGE REDWAY, YORK STREET, COVENT GARDEN.

The Path:

A magazine devoted to the Brotherhood of Humanity, Theosophy
in America, and the Study of Occult Science, Philosophy,
and Aryan literature.

EDITED BY

WILLIAM Q. JUDGE.

(Published under the auspices of The Aryan Theosophical
Society of New York.)

Monthly. Subscription, 10s. per annum.

GEORGE REDWAY, YORK STREET, COVENT GARDEN.

INDEX.

CPSIA information can be obtained at www.ICGtesting.com
Printed in the USA
BVOW03s1113170215

388072BV00016B/281/P